Embellished Crochet

Embellished Crochet

Bead, Embroider, Fringe, and More

28 STUNNING DESIGNS TO MAKE
USING CARON INTERNATIONAL YARN

Cari Clement

ST. MARTIN'S GRIFFIN

NEW YORK

PHOTOGRAPHY BY Jack Deutsch

TECHNICAL EDITORS: Barb Sunderlage, Karen J. Hay, and Dee Neer

BOOK DESIGN BY Georgia Rucker Design

HAIR AND MAKEUP BY Laly Zambrana

CHARTS AND ILLUSTRATIONS BY Dee Neer

CONTRIBUTORS INCLUDE: Kim Biddex, Gayle Bunn, Cari Clement, Noreen Crone-Findlay, Lisa Gonzales, Tammy Hildebrand, Candi Jensen, Marilyn Losee, Treva McCain, Kim Rutledge, Susan Shildmyer, Heidi Stepp, and Margaret Willson.

www.stmartins.com

LIBRARY OF CONGRESS CATALOGING-IN-PUBLICATION DATA
Clement, Cari.
    Embellished crochet: bead, embroider, fringe, and more: 28 stunning designs to make using Caron International Yarn / Cari Clement. — 1st ed.
        p. cm.
    ISBN-13: 978-0-312-36439-7
    ISBN-10: 0-312-36439-3

  1. Crocheting--Patterns. 2. Fancy work. I. Title.

TT825.C63255 2007

746.43'4041--dc22   2007021177

First Edition: November 2007

10 9 8 7 6 5 4 3 2 1

THIS BOOK IS DEDICATED TO ALL THE YOUNG CROCHETERS AT THE
IMBABAZI ORPHANAGE IN GISENYI, WHERE I VISIT WHEN I GO TO RWANDA.

p. 34

contents

p. 52

p. 76

p. 94

p. 110

p. 144

foreword

BY NICKY EPSTEIN

When my longtime friend, Cari Clement, asked if I would consider writing the foreword to her book, *Embellished Crochet,* I said, "Of course!" Whether it's embellishing on, over, or beyond edges, embellishing for me is what makes a garment truly special, a signature the creator gives to her garment that makes it uniquely hers. While many crocheters can use the same basic stitch pattern to make a garment, adding a touch of embellishing can change a garment's look dramatically and beautifully. It's the addition of just a few beads, some embroidery touches, a tassel, beaded fringe—simple and easy techniques—that make the garment special.

The projects in this book are just right—not too much embellishing, not too few added accents. They range from the super-easy to the more challenging, encouraging you to learn as you create. What's so wonderful about them is their simplicity of silhouette—allowing the embellishing to make them stand-out pieces. These designs also inspire you to incorporate the techniques learned from making them into other projects down the road.

I am honored to have been asked to write this foreword, and I feel the designers featured in *Embellished Crochet* should really be complimented for their amazing creativity, attention to detail, and willingness to dive into the expanding world of embellishing, headfirst.

introduction

The word "embellished" denotes a certain unique and very special individual type of creativity given to a garment. Nothing could be truer of the embellishing incorporated into the designs in this book: there are as many takes on the word as there are designers, and their talent and exacting attention to every detail is apparent in the amazing works of art they've created.

I initially planned to create a pattern book, but as the designs began to arrive, I realized that technique descriptions, photographs, and charts would be necessary to enable readers to better understand

the techniques used, and often created, by each designer. So this book has evolved into a combination of pattern *and* technique—two books in one!

The techniques used by a number of patterns throughout are described in Basic Techniques. All the other embellishing techniques that are unique to the individual patterns are shown in photographs and have detailed step-by-step instructions with the appropriate patterns.

The yarns in this book are as versatile as the techniques. Simply Soft is an exceptionally great yarn for bead crochet due to its size (light 4-ply), its smoothness (beads slide on well), and its ability to be easily split into two 2-plies for use in traditional and bead embroidery. And the colors are ideal for so many of the projects. Other Caron yarns, such as Bliss and Glimmer, also lend themselves especially well to the techniques employed by the designers.

But one of the things I like most about the designs in this book is how versatile the embellishing applications are. You can take a medallion, an embroidery stitch, a bead motif, or a stitch/embroidery combination and apply them to just about any project, making it a truly couturelike creation.

So have fun, enjoy the adventure, and crochet away!

Basic Techniques

These are techniques that are used throughout this book. Check the instructions for the project you are doing to determine if it incorporates any of these and, if so, take a few minutes to learn the steps.

INTEGRAL EMBELLISHING: BEAD CROCHET

While embellishing is usually reserved for the "finishing" section of a pattern, crocheting beads *into* a garment is really a separate technique from embellishing that often uses beads as applied accents.

There are many types of bead crochet stitches, ranging from at what point a bead is placed into the stitch to the type of stitch into which a bead is placed, and how frequently the beads are added. Bead crochet is usually worked on a wrong-side row, so that the bead will be on the right side of the fabric when the row is completed.

There are five different types of bead crochet used throughout this book:

- bead chain
- bead single crochet
- bead half-double crochet
- bead double crochet
- bead slip stitch

Each of these techniques is described below, and will be referred to in the pattern instructions. While there are several different ways to execute each of these techniques, usually at what point in executing the stitch the bead is slid down to the hook, we wanted to keep this book as easy-to-follow as possible, so only those techniques used in the pattern instructions are described here.

BEAD CHAIN (BC)

Note: There may be a bead on every chain or every other chain or whatever spacing the designer calls for in the pattern instructions.

1. Thread the yarn with the appropriate number of beads.
2. Begin by making a slip knot on hook; yarn over hook and pull up a loop (first chain).
3. Slide down a bead as close to the hook as it can go.
4. Yarn over and pull through a loop one; chain worked after the bead.
5. Continue in this manner, working the number of chains indicated in the instructions between each bead.

BEAD SINGLE CROCHET (BSC)

Note: There may be a beaded stitch for every stitch, every other stitch or however many beads the designer calls for on a single row. This is also true for bead double crochet and bead slip st.

1. Thread the yarn with the appropriate number of beads.
2. Work the foundation chain as indicated.
3. Work in stitch pattern until you reach the first row using beads.
4. Insert hook in next stitch, yarn over and pull up a loop.
5. Slide a bead down as close to the hook as it can go.
6. Yarn over and draw through both loops on hook (bsc) or all 3 loops on hook (bhdc); one stitch has been worked, with the bead enclosed in the stitch.
7. Continue in this manner, working the number of stitches indicated in the instructions between each bead.

BEAD DOUBLE CROCHET (BDC)

1. Thread the yarn with the appropriate number of beads.
2. Work the foundation chain as indicated.
3. Work in stitch pattern until you reach the first row using beads.
4. Yarn over hook.
5. Insert hook in next stitch, yarn over and pull up a loop.
6. Slide a bead down, as close to the hook as it can go.
7. (Yarn over and draw through two loops) twice; one bdc has been worked, with the bead enclosed in the stitch.
8. Continue in this manner, working the number of stitches indicated in the instructions between each bead.

BEAD HALF-DOUBLE CROCHET (BHDC)

1. Thread the yarn with the appropriate number of beads.
2. Work the foundation chain as indicated.
3. Work in stitch pattern until you reach the first row using beads.
4. Yarn over hook.
5. Insert hook in next stitch, yarn over and pull up a loop.
6. Slide a bead down as close to the hook as it can go.
7. Yarn over and draw through both loops on hook all 3 loops on hook; one stitch has been worked, with the bead enclosed in the stitch.
8. Continue in this manner, working the number of stitches indicated in the instructions between each bead.

BEAD SLIP STITCH (BSS)

1. Thread the yarn with the appropriate number of beads.
2. Work the foundation chain as indicated.
3. Work in stitch pattern until you reach the first row using beads.
4. Insert hook into next stitch.
5. Slide a bead down, as close to the hook as it can go.
6. Yarn over and draw through the stitch and the loop on hook; one slip stitch has been worked, with the bead enclosed in the stitch.
7. Continue in this manner, working the number of slip stitches indicated in the instructions between each bead.

BEADS AND BEADING TOOLS

Beads come in an almost mind-numbing variety of shapes and sizes, but what, to me, seems to be more important for both bead crochet and bead embellishing is the size of the bead's hole. This determines whether or not you can thread yarn or sewing thread through the bead and what tool you will need to do so. Since beads come in such a variety, I felt it best not to display any here but to focus on the tools you'll need for various projects in this book.

Beads' outer dimensions are sized in millimeters (mm), but the holes are *not* sized, so it's important to know if the bead you'd like to use can be worked using the technique the pattern calls for. Mostly, it's just a matter of "eyeballing" the bead's hole, but if you're ordering beads by mail, be sure the catalog company shows a side view of the bead's hole before you order. In cases where there are lots of the same bead used or where I felt the bead may be hard to find, I've listed the name and item number of the bead and the bead manufacturer and listed its Web site (see "Resources" at the back of this book). With the increasing popularity of using beads in knitting and crochet, there are more and more beads with ample-sized holes that are quite suitable for bead crochet.

Obviously you'll need a crochet hook for the basic construction of the garment. But when it comes to beads, the only size hook suggested in this book (other than for bead crochet) is a size 11 steel hook.

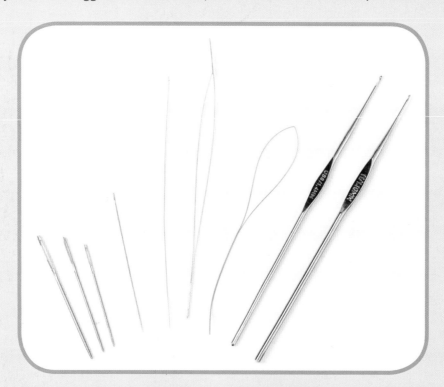

FROM LEFT TO RIGHT IN THE ABOVE PHOTO ARE:

1. Three sizes of tapestry needles, from size 16—22 (the higher the number, the smaller the needle). These are also used for the embroidery found in this book.

2. A traditional small-eye beading needle.

3. A large-eye beading needle made from two small wires twisted together (not good for sewing through crocheted fabric, but helpful for making beaded fringes, etc.).

4. A "large eye" beading needle (made from two pieces of wire soldered together, leaving a very long "eye.") This needle can be used to sew through crocheted fabric as long as it's not too densely crocheted.

5. A dental floss threader. This is one of my favorite tools to use—not only is it widely available and very cheap, but it threads beads onto yarn quite well.

6. Steel crochet hooks used to insert into beads and hook a loop of sewing thread that is pulled through a small-holed bead.

SPLITTING HAIRS—ER, YARN

A number of patterns in this book call for splitting 4-ply yarn into two 2-plies—even four single plies, primarily used for embroidery and beading.

This is quite simple, as you can see in the photo above.

1. Wind off the length of 4-ply yarn called for in the pattern.

2. Leaving approximately 1 yard free, wind the remaining yarn into a loose ball.

3. Secure the ball with a yarn needle to hold the ball intact, or attach a clip to the ball for weight, as shown above.

4. Separate the unsecured yarn end into two 2-ply strands, allowing the ball to spin freely.

5. Wind each 2-ply strand onto an embroidery floss bobbin.

6. Release another yard of yarn from the ball, secure it again with the yarn needle or clip.

7. Repeat Steps 4—6 until the entire length of yarn has been separated into 2-ply strands.

8. If the pattern calls for a single ply, you can repeat the above process with a 2-ply strand to get two single-ply strands, but be aware that these are fragile and can pull apart easily, so treat them gently.

IMPORTANT NOTES TO PATTERNS

- Patterns are written with *suggested* crochet hook sizes. *Be sure* to check your gauge before beginning a project, using the hook size that achieves the gauge.

- Difficulty ratings are for the difficulty level of crochet, not for embellishing. Some projects will be easy to crochet and easy to embellish, others easy to crochet but more challenging to embellish. Be sure to read through the pattern ahead of time to note the embellishing required.

- Schematics given are for the actual size of the crocheted pieces *before* they are assembled. They are *not* finished measurements, which will differ from schematics measurements.

- While all of our readers have heard this many times, I cannot emphasize the importance of testing for gauge. It may not matter for wraps, purses, scarves and shawls, but to achieve not only a good fit but the right look for your project, be sure to check the gauge.

- Also, if you are using yarns with a dye lot printed on the label, be sure to purchase enough yarn of the same dye lot to complete your garment.

IMPORTANT NOTES ABOUT THE CARE OF YOUR EMBELLISHED PROJECT

Most, but not all, of the yarns used in *Embellished Crochet* are machine washable and dryable. Be sure to check the label on the yarn before you wash or dry your garment. However, if you have used glass beads that could break or get scratched in a washing machine and dryer, consider hand washing the garment and rolling it in a towel to get out most of the moisture, then laying flat to dry. Some beads can also snag yarn, so also take care when washing these garments—and try to choose beads without uneven or irregular edges.

So now you're well-armed to begin your journey through *Embellished Crochet*! Have fun!

Focus on Color

Think deep, saturated colors...
bright, sparkling colors...
intense, eye-popping colors...

Beaded Ruffled Shrug

DESIGNED BY KIM RUTLEDGE

INTERMEDIATE

Bliss is the perfect yarn for this embellishing technique using beads. The super-soft, slightly fuzzy nature of Bliss totally disguises the thread and the dangle-bead technique easily shows off the beads. The technique is easy, takes little time, and results in a young, unique look.

SIZES
Small (Medium/Large)

FINISHED MEASUREMENTS
To fit Bust 32 – 35 (36 – 39)"/81 – 89 (91.5 – 99) cm
Back Length 17 (18)"/43 (45.5) cm, including ruffle

YARN
Caron International's Bliss (60% acrylic, 40% nylon; 1.76 oz/50 g, 82 yds/75 m ball):

• #0008 Sour Apple, 10 (11) balls

CROCHET HOOK
One size US K-10.5 (6.5 mm), or size to obtain gauge

ADDITIONAL MATERIALS
502 (570) – 6 mm Lime Glass Miracle Beads
Beading needle (thin enough to fit through bead)

Beading nylon or beading thread to match
Yarn needle
Row counter (optional)

GAUGE
In stitch pattern, 12 sts and 8 rows = 4"/10 cm

CROCHET STITCHES USED
ch: chain
hdc: half double crochet
sc: single crochet
slip st: slip stitch

NOTE
Shrug is worked in one piece; beads are added before assembly, allowing the option of adding as many or as few beads as preferred.

SHRUG
Chain 155 (171).

Row 1 (RS): Hdc in third ch from hook, hdc in next ch, * ch 1, skip 1 ch, hdc in next ch; repeat from * across to last 3 ch, ch 1, skip 1 ch, hdc in each of last 2 ch, turn—78 (86) hdc.

Row 2: Ch 3 (counts as hdc, ch-1), skip first 2 hdc, * hdc in next ch-1 space, ch 1, skip next hdc; repeat from * to last hdc, hdc in last hdc, turn.

Row 3: Ch 2 (counts as hdc), * hdc in next ch-1 space, ch 1, skip next hdc; repeat from * across, end hdc in last ch-1 space and in last hdc, turn.

Rows 4 – 27: Repeat Rows 2 and 3.

Size Small: Fasten off.

Size Medium/Large, work 3 more rows, ending with Row 2. Fasten off. Using yarn needle, weave in ends.

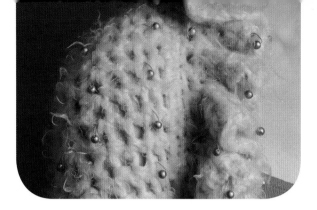

FINISHING

EMBELLISHING

Note: Add beads to body of Shrug before assembling.

Thread the tapestry needle with the beading thread.

1. With RS facing, beginning Row 2 (see Bead Placement Chart, page 21), secure beading yarn to WS of piece.

2. Thread needle through the first hdc on the WS of piece.

3. Bring needle to RS at Point A (see Attach Bead Illustration).

4. Thread one bead onto thread.

5. Holding bead down, insert needle through Point B to the WS of the piece, leaving the bead on a loop of beading thread long enough so that the bead hangs down to the ch-1 space on the row below.

6. Bring needle to the RS at Point C, then to WS at Point D, which secures the loop in place.

7. Thread needle through the next hdc, to hide the thread.

8. Repeat Steps 4—8, referring to Row 2 of Bead Placement Chart.

Tip: Give a lengthwise tug on the shrug to be sure you're not pulling the beading nylon or thread too tightly and gathering the stitches.

9. Thread needle through the backs of two rows, using the same method as for Step 8.

10. Repeat Steps 3—8 for the next and every third row.

ASSEMBLY

SLEEVE SEAMS

Fold shrug in half lengthwise with WS tog.

Measure and mark 17 (17 ½)"/43(44) cm from each end (see diagram on page 21).

Sew seams, leaving 18 (21 ¾)"/46(55) cm open in center.

RUFFLE — CUFFS

Work around each Cuff.

Round 1: With RS facing, join yarn with slip st at seam; ch 1, sc an odd number of sts evenly around, join with slip st in first sc.

Round 2: Ch 1, sc in each sc around, join with slip st in first sc.

Round 3: Ch 3 (counts as hdc, ch 1), * skip 1 sc, hdc in next sc, ch 1; repeat from * around, end skip last sc, join with slip st in first hdc.

Round 4: Slip st in first ch-1 space, ch 3, hdc in same ch-1 space, * ch 1, skip next hdc, [hdc, ch 1, hdc] in next ch-1 space; repeat from * around, end ch 1, skip next hdc, join with slip st in first st.

Round 5: Repeat Round 4.

Round 6: Slip st in first ch-1 space, ch 3, hdc in same ch-1 space, * ch 1, skip next hdc, hdc in next ch-1 space, ch 1, skip next hdc, [hdc, ch 1, hdc] in next ch-1 space; repeat from * around, end ch 1, join with slip st to first hdc. Fasten off Cuffs.

RUFFLE — COLLAR

Work around center opening for Collar.

Rounds 1–6: As above. Repeat Round 3 once. Fasten off Collar. Weave in all ends.

BEADING — CUFFS AND COLLAR

Work bead loops as for Shrug, working on every third hdc (skipping two hdc between each bead loop), across the last round only of the Cuffs and Collar.

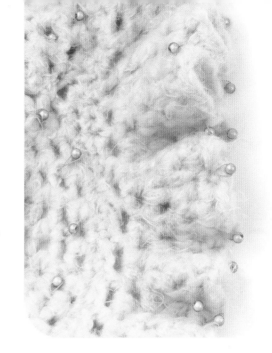

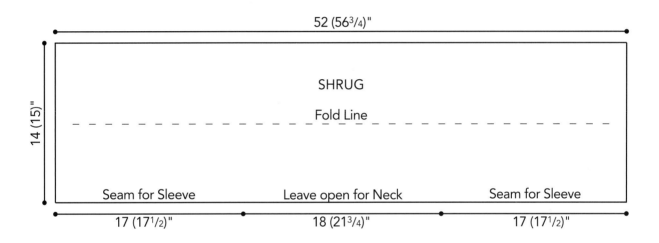

BEAD PLACEMENT CHART

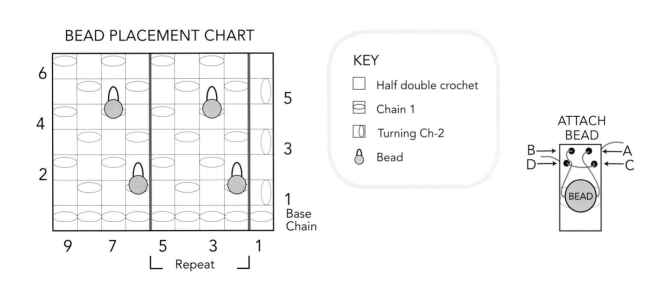

KEY

▢ Half double crochet

⬭ Chain 1

◖ Turning Ch-2

⬭ Bead

ATTACH BEAD

Mini-Squares Wrap

DESIGNED BY KIM BIDDEX WITH MARILYN LOSEE

This colorful wrap is the perfect way to top off a summer dress or liven up a winter coat. The beautiful embroidery embellishing is easy to do and makes this Simply Soft wrap a real eye-catcher!

ONE SIZE

FINISHED MEASUREMENTS

Width 15"/38 cm

Length 61"/155 cm, excluding fringe

YARN

Caron International's Simply Soft
(100% acrylic; 6 oz/170 g, 315 yds/288 m skein):

- #9742 Grey Heather (MC), 1 skein

Caron International's Simply Soft Brites
(100% acrylic; 6 oz/170 g, 315 yds/288 m skein):

- #9604 Watermelon (A), 1 skein
- #9608 Blue Mint (B), 1 skein
- #9610 Grape (C), 1 skein
- #9607 Limelight (D), 1 skein
- #9606 Lemonade (E), 1 skein
- #9605 Mango (F), 1 skein

CROCHET HOOK

One size US H-8 (5 mm), or size to obtain gauge

ADDITIONAL MATERIALS

Yarn/tapestry needle size 13 or 16

GAUGE

In single crochet, 16 rows = 4"/10 cm; each square = 2 ½"/6.25 cm

CROCHET STITCHES USED

ch: chain

dc: double crochet

sc: single crochet

slip st: slip stitch

NOTE

Make 108 squares, 18 each using colors A, B, C, D, E, and F.

SQUARES

Using appropriate color, chain 3.

Round 1: Work 2 dc in third ch from hook (counts as first cluster), ch 1; in same ch, work [3 dc, ch 1] 3 times, join with slip st to top of beginning ch-3—4 dc clusters.

Round 2: Ch 3, * work [3 dc, ch 1, 3 dc] in next ch-1 space, ch 1; repeat from * 2 times, end by working [3 dc, ch 1, 2 dc] in last ch-1 space, join with slip st to second ch of beginning ch-3. Fasten off.

ASSEMBLY

Using yarn needle and appropriate color(s), join Squares in rows of 6, then join rows to form a rectangle as shown (see Assembly Diagram).

BORDERS

(work on both ends of rectangle)

With RS facing, using MC, join yarn with a slip st to corner on one short end of piece.

Row 1: Ch 1, sc evenly across, working 9 sc across each Square; turn—54 sc.

Row 2: Ch 1, sc in each sc across; turn.

Repeat Row 2 until Border measures 8"/20.5 cm from beginning. Fasten off.

FINISHING

Using yarn/tapestry needle, weave in all ends.

EMBELLISHING

Note: Embellishing is worked on both sides, making the Borders reversible. References to WS and RS are for clarity of instructions only. Use photo and illustrations as guides for placement of Vine, Flowers, and Leaves.

FLOWERS

(make 20: 4 each using A, B, C, E, and F)

1. Leaving a 6"/15 cm tail for attaching Flower to Wrap, chain 3.

2. Work 2 dc in third ch from hook, ch 2, slip st in third ch (first petal made); in the same ch, work [ch 2, 2 dc, ch 2, slip st] four times— 5 petals. Fasten off.

3. Sew 10 Flowers randomly to each border, 5 on RS, 5 on WS opposite those on RS.

VINE

Work on both borders of Wrap.

1. Thread tapestry needle with one strand of D.

2. Referring to Border Embroidery/Flowers illustration for stitch placement, work ¼"/.6 cm Running stitches between the flowers (stitches show alternately on both sides of the work).

3. Work Whip stitch through the Running stitches on both sides of the Border. (**Note:** The arrows in the Assembly Diagram show the path of the Whip stitch through the Running stitches.)

LEAVES

1. Thread tapestry needle with a double strand of D.

2. * Insert needle at Point A (see Leaf Illustration) through the border to the WS, then bring needle to the RS at Point B, 1" to 1 ½"/2.5 to 3.5 cm from the entry point. Work loosely to allow leaf shape to form on both RS and WS of piece.

3. Repeat from * 3 or 4 times, until the leaf is the desired shape and thickness. Fasten off securely and weave ends into Leaf.

FRINGE

1. Cut 16"/41 cm -long strands of A, B, C, D, E, and F.

2. Holding 2 strands of one color together, fold the strands in half lengthwise.

3. Using crochet hook, * insert hook from WS to RS into corner st of Border, pull through

fold of strands (loop), insert ends into loop, and pull tight against edge of Border.

4. Repeat from * in color sequence of A, B, C, D, E, F, or as desired, working into every sc along last row of Border.

5. Trim Fringe ends even.

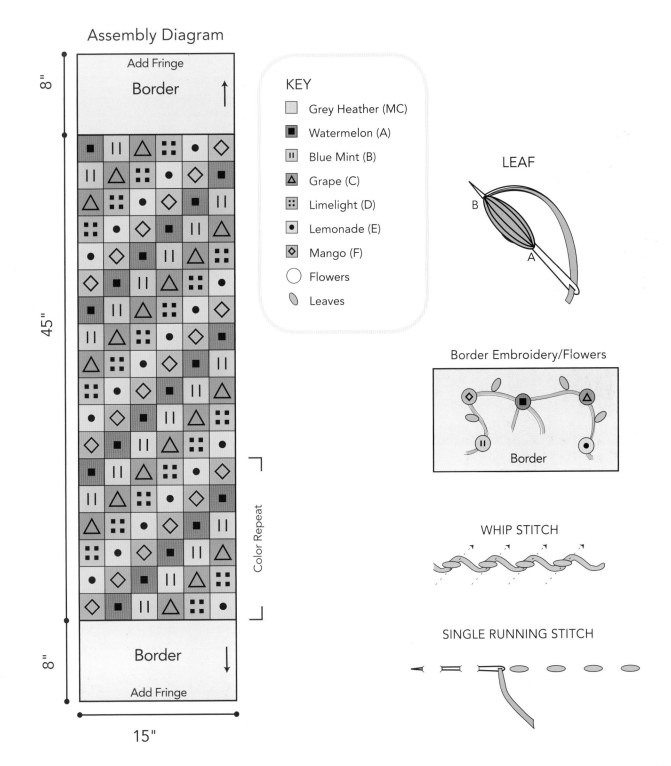

Assembly Diagram

Add Fringe

Border

8"

45"

Color Repeat

Border

Add Fringe

8"

15"

KEY

- Grey Heather (MC)
- Watermelon (A)
- Blue Mint (B)
- Grape (C)
- Limelight (D)
- Lemonade (E)
- Mango (F)
- Flowers
- Leaves

LEAF

Border Embroidery/Flowers

Border

WHIP STITCH

SINGLE RUNNING STITCH

Tulips Shawl

DESIGNED BY TREVA G. MCCAIN

INTERMEDIATE

Crochet provides the perfect background for embellishments of all kinds. Cross stitch with beads makes a bold statement on this truly elegant shawl. Simply Soft provides the drape and intense color that creates an impressive piece.

ONE SIZE

FINISHED MEASUREMENTS

Width 68"/ 172.5 cm

Length 44"/112 cm

YARN

Caron International's Simply Soft Brites (100% acrylic; 6 oz/170 g, 315 yds/288 m skein):

- #9727 Black (MC), 4 skeins
- #9610 Grape (A), 1 skein
- #9608 Blue Mint (B), 1 skein
- #9609 Berry Blue (C), 1 skein

CROCHET HOOK

One size US I-9 (5.5 mm), or size to obtain gauge

ADDITIONAL MATERIALS

Yarn needle

30 g tube #3 seed rocaille beads in mixed shades of blue and purple, 2 tubes

Beading needle thin enough to fit through beads

GAUGE

Gauge is not critical in this project.

CROCHET STITCHES USED

ch: chain

dc: double crochet

sc: single crochet

sc2tog: single crochet 2 together—insert hook in next stitch, yarn over and pull up loop (two loops on hook), insert hook in next stitch, yarn over and pull up a loop, yarn over and draw through all three loops on hook.

slip st: slip stitch

Mesh Stitch (multiple of 2 sts + 1)

NOTE: Each mesh (st) is made up of one dc and a ch-1; the last dc completes the final mesh (st).

ROW 1: Ch 4 (counts as dc, ch 1), dc in next st (first mesh) [ch1, dc], repeat from [to] across, working final dc in last st, turn.

Repeat Row 1 for Mesh st.

NOTES

1. Tulip Square is worked first, then embroidered in beaded Cross stitch, using the Chart; mesh side panels are worked separately and attached to upper two sides of the Square. An additional mesh panel is worked at the upper edge to complete Shawl.

2. Each square on the Chart represents one beaded Cross stitch on the Tulip Square.

HELPFUL

Using a strand of contrast-color thread or yarn, work a Basting st from corner to corner in both directions on the Tulip Square; these lines correspond to the red lines on the Chart, and indicate where to center the Tulip Motif.

TULIP SQUARE

Using MC, chain 2.

Row 1: Work 3 sc in second ch from hook, turn—3 sc.

Row 2: Ch 1, work 2 sc in first sc (increase), sc in next sc, work 2 sc in last sc (increase), turn—5 sc.

Row 3: Ch 1, work 2 sc in first sc, sc in each sc across to last sc, work 2 sc in last sc, turn—7 sc.

Rows 4 – 40: Repeat Row 3—81 sc.

Row 41: Sc2tog, sc in each space across to last 2 sc, sc2tog, turn—79 sc remain.

Rows 42 – 79: Repeat Row 41—3 sc remain.

Row 80: Sc3tog—1 sc remains; do NOT fasten off.

BORDER

With RS facing, working into last sc worked (corner), ch 1, * work 3 sc in corner sc, sc in each row end to next corner; repeat from * around, join with a slip st to beginning sc. Fasten off. Using yarn needle, weave in all ends.

TULIP MOTIF

1. Working in Cross st from Chart and photos above, cross-stitch the Tulip Motif.

2. For the cross-stitched areas with beads, separate a length of desired yarn into a 2-ply strand (see page 15), thread beading needle, and secure yarn to WS, bringing up needle to begin the first stitch.

3. Slide 2 beads onto needle and slide down next to square when making the first leg of your Cross stitch (/).

4. Slide 3 beads onto needle and slide down next to square when finishing second leg of Cross stitch (\ ).

MESH PANELS (MAKE 2)

Using MC, chain 5.

Row 1: Dc in the fifth ch from hook — this is the first ch worked (counts as dc, ch 1, dc)—1 mesh.

Row 2: Ch 4 (counts as dc, ch 1), dc in first dc (second ch of beginning ch-5), ch 1, skip next ch, [dc, ch 1, dc] in 4th ch of beginning ch-5, turn— 3 meshes.

Row 3: Ch 4 (counts as dc, ch 1), dc in first dc (increase), ch 1, skip ch-1 space, work [dc, ch 1] in each dc across to last dc (third ch of beginning ch-4), [dc, ch 1, dc] in last dc (increase), turn— 5 meshes.

Rows 4 – 20: Repeat Row 3, increasing 1 mesh st each side every row—39 meshes.

Fasten off, leaving a 20"/51 cm tail. Using yarn needle and tail, sew one Mesh Panel to each upper side edge of Tulip Square. Weave in ends.

UPPER EDGE

With RS facing, attach yarn to first dc (corner) of right-hand side Mesh Panel, ready to work across the upper edge.

Row 1: Ch 4 (counts as dc, ch-1), dc in same space as joining (increase), ch 1, skip ch-1 space, work [dc, ch 1] in each dc across to last st, work [dc, ch 1, dc] in last st (increase), turn— 80 meshes.

Rows 2 – 18: Repeat Row 3 of Mesh Panels, increasing 1 mesh st each side every row— 114 meshes.

BORDER

Round 1 (RS): Working across the upper edge, ch 3 (counts as first dc), work 2 dc in first dc (upper right-hand corner); dc in each dc and ch-1 space across to last dc; work 5 dc in last dc (upper left-hand corner); work 3 dc in each row end along side of Mesh Panel; dc in each sc along side of Tulip Square to lower edge (point of Tulip Square); work 3 dc in center st at point; dc in each sc along side of Tulip Square; work 3 dc in each row end along side of Mesh Panel to upper right-hand corner; work 2 dc in same st as first st, join with a slip st in beginning ch-3, turn.

Round 2: Ch 3 (counts as dc), work 2 dc in same space as joining (upper right-hand corner), dc in each dc around, working 3 dc in the center dc at lower edge point, and 5 dc in center st at upper left-hand corner; end by working 2 dc in same st as first st, join with a slip st in beginning ch-3, turn.

Rounds 3 – 5: Repeat Round 2.

Round 6: Ch 1, work 3 sc in same space as joining, sc in each dc around, working 3 sc in the center dc at lower point, and 5 sc in center dc at upper corner; end by working 2 sc in same st as first st, join with a slip st in beginning ch-1, turn.

Round 7: Ch 1, sc in same space as joining, ch 1, [sc, ch 1] in each sc across upper edge to center st of sc-5 (corner); * ch 5, skip 4 sc, work 2 sc in next st; repeat from * around, working [sc, ch 5, sc] in center st at lower edge point, join with a slip st to beginning sc at upper edge corner. Fasten off.

FINISHING

Using yarn needle, weave in ends.

FRINGE

Cut strands 16"/41 cm long; holding 6 strands together, fold Fringe in half. Using crochet hook, * insert hook from WS to RS into first ch-5 space, pull through fold of stands (loop), insert ends into loop and pull tight against edge, repeat from *, working into each ch-5 space around.

* Separate each 12-strand Fringe into two 6-strand groups; combine one 6-strand group with the adjacent group from the next Fringe (see illustration). Tie an overhand knot in new 12-strand group, approximately 2"/5 cm down from the edge of Shawl; repeat from * across, leaving one 6-strand group free at each side.

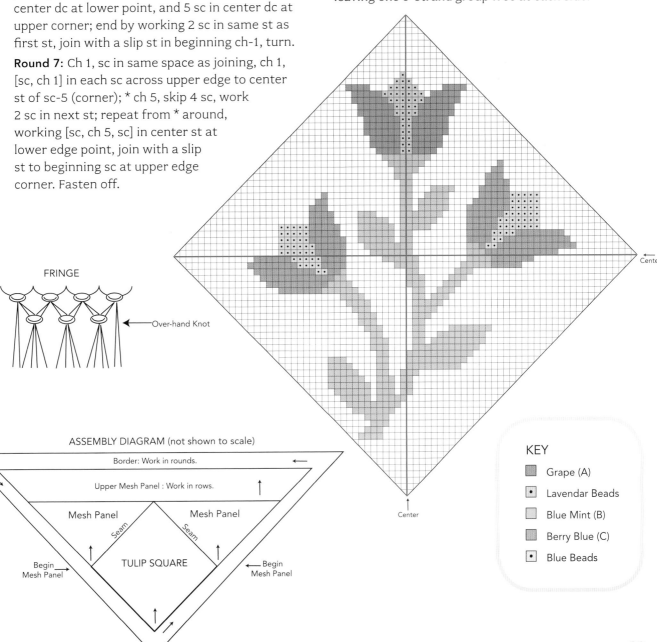

FRINGE

Over-hand Knot

ASSEMBLY DIAGRAM (not shown to scale)

Border: Work in rounds.

Upper Mesh Panel : Work in rows.

Mesh Panel

Mesh Panel

Seam

Seam

TULIP SQUARE

Begin Mesh Panel

Begin Mesh Panel

Center

Center

KEY

- Grape (A)
- Lavendar Beads
- Blue Mint (B)
- Berry Blue (C)
- Blue Beads

Gypsy Skirt

DESIGNED BY TREVA G. MCCAIN

INTERMEDIATE

This versatile skirt can be worn year-round and is the ideal design for experimenting with color. The bands separating the tiers make great "canvases" for different types of embroidery and embellishing. Simply Soft gives the skirt the perfect drape.

SIZES

Small (Medium, Large)

FINISHED MEASUREMENTS

Waist 25 (31, 37)"/63.5 (78.5, 94) cm

Length 32"/81 cm, all sizes

YARN

Caron International's Simply Soft
(100% acrylic; 6 oz/170 g, 315 yds/288 m skein):

- #9707 Dark Sage (MC), 3 (3, 4) skeins
- #9705 Sage (A), 1 skein
- #9723 Raspberry (B), 1 skein
- #9721 Victorian Rose (C), 1 skein
- #9710 Country Blue (D), 1 skein
- #9709 Lt. Country Blue (E), 1 skein

CROCHET HOOK

One size US I-9 (5.5 mm), or size to obtain gauge

ADDITIONAL MATERIALS

Yarn needle

30 g tube frosted green #3 seed beads, 1 tube

Beading needle (thin enough to fit through beads)

GAUGE

In Shell pattern, 4 shell-and-dc groups = 5"/12.5 cm; 10 rows = 5"/12.5 cm

SPECIAL TERMS

Shell: Work (2 dc, ch 1, 2 dc) in stitch indicated.

Picot: Ch 5, sc in fifth ch from hook.

CROCHET STITCHES USED

ch: chain

dc: double crochet

picot—ch 5, sc in fifth ch from hook.

sc: single crochet

shell—work (2 dc, ch 1, 2 dc) in stitch indicated.

slip st: slip stitch

SKIRT

Using MC, beginning at waist, chain 120 (150, 180); join with a slip st to form a ring, being careful not to twist chain.

Round 1: Ch 1, sc in same space as joining and in each ch around; join with a slip st to beginning sc—120 (150, 180) sc.

Round 2: Ch 4 (counts as first dc, ch 1), * skip 1 st, dc in next st, ch 1; repeat from * around, join with a slip st in third ch of beginning ch-4—60 (75, 90) dc.

Round 3: Ch 1, sc in same space and in each dc and ch-1 space around, join with a slip st to beginning sc—120 (150, 180) sc.

Round 4: Begin Shell pattern—Ch 3 (counts as first dc here and throughout), skip 2 st, shell in next st, skip 2 sts, * dc in next st, skip 2 sts, shell in next st, skip 2 sts; repeat from * around, join with a slip st in third ch of beginning ch-3—20 (25, 30) shells, 20 (25, 30) dc.

Round 5: Ch 3; skip 2 dc, shell in ch-1 space, skip 2 dc, * dc in next dc, skip 2 dc, shell in ch-1 space, skip 2 dc; repeat from * around, join with a slip st in third ch of beginning ch-3.

Rounds 6 – 13: Repeat Round 5.

Round 14: Ch 1, sc in same space and in each dc and ch-1 space around, join with a slip st to beginning sc—120 (150, 180) sc.

Round 15: Ch 1, sc in same space and in each sc around, join with a slip st to beginning sc.

Rounds 16 – 21: Repeat Round 15.

Round 22: Increase Round — Ch 1, sc in same space and in each of the next 3 sc, * work 2 sc in next sc, sc in each of the next 4 sc; repeat from * to around, end work 2 sc in last sc, join with a slip st to beginning sc—144 (180, 216) sc.

Round 23: Repeat Round 4—24 (30, 36) shells, 24 (30, 36) dc.

Rounds 24 – 34: Repeat Round 5.

Round 35: Repeat Round 14—144 (180, 216) sc.

Rounds 36 – 42: Repeat Round 15.

Round 43: Increase Round — Ch 1, sc in same space and in each of the next 4 sc, * work 2 sc in next sc, sc in each of the next 5 sc; repeat from * around, end work 2 sc in last sc, join with a slip st to beginning sc—168 (210, 252) sc.

Round 44: Repeat Round 4—28 (35, 42) shells; 28 (35, 42) dc.

Rounds 45 – 55: Repeat Round 5.

Round 56: Repeat Round 14—168 (210, 252) sc.

Rounds 57 – 63: Repeat Round 15.

Round 64: Increase Round — Ch 1, sc in same space and in each of the next 5 sc, * work 2 sc in next sc; sc in each of the next 6 sc; repeat from * around, end work 2 sc in last sc, join with a slip st to beginning sc—192 (240, 288) sc.

Round 65: Repeat Round 4—32 (40, 48) shells, 32 (40, 48) dc.

Rounds 66 – 76: Repeat Round 5.

EDGING

Ch 1, sc in same space, skip 2 dc, work [3 dc, picot, 3 dc] in ch-1 space, skip 2 dc, * sc in next dc, skip 2 dc, work [3 dc, picot, 3 dc] in next ch-1 space, skip 2 dc; repeat from * around, join with a slip st to beginning sc. Fasten off.

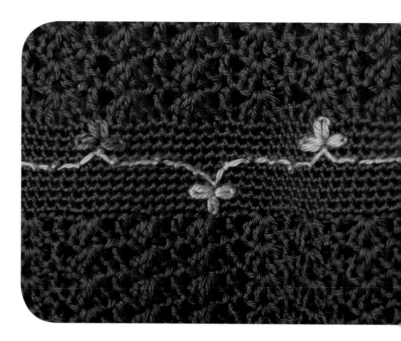

EMBELLISHING

EMBROIDERY

1. **Flowers:** Using B, C, D, and E, referring to photo as a guide for color placement, embroider 12 to 14 evenly spaced 3-petal flowers on each sc band of Skirt, using Lazy Daisy stitch (see Illustration and photo).

2. **Vine:** Separate a 36" to 42"/92 to 107 cm length of A into 2-ply strands (see page 15). Using a 2-ply strand of A, embroider vine (see Embroidery Diagram and photo), adding beads as shown.

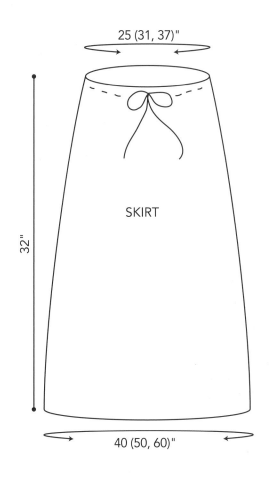

25 (31, 37)"

SKIRT

32"

40 (50, 60)"

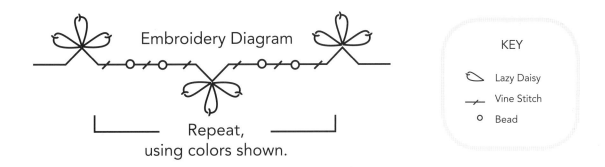

Embroidery Diagram

Repeat,
using colors shown.

KEY

🐦 Lazy Daisy

╱ Vine Stitch

○ Bead

Step 1

Step 2

Completed
Daisy Loop

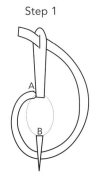

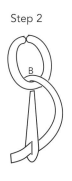

LAZY DAISY STITCH

Flower Wrap

DESIGNED BY KIM RUTLEDGE

EXPERIENCED

The flowers really "pop" against the black base of this spectacular design. The base is crocheted first, then the flowers and beads are attached to create this dramatic but playful look.

ONE SIZE

FINISHED MEASUREMENTS

Width 84"/213 cm

Length 32"/81 cm (upper edge to point)

YARN

Caron International's Simply Soft
(100% acrylic; 6 oz/ 170 g, 315 yds/288 m skein):

- #9727 Black (MC), 3 skeins

Caron International's Simply Soft Brites
(100% acrylic; 6 oz/170 g, 315 yds/288 m skein):

- #9604 Watermelon (A), 1 skein
- #9605 Mango (B), 1 skein
- #9606 Lemonade (C), 1 skein
- #9607 Limelight (D), 1 skein

CROCHET HOOKS

One each size US I-9 (5.5 mm) and US G-6 (4 mm), or size to obtain gauge

ADDITIONAL MATERIALS

Yarn needle

Pony beads 4 x 7 mm: 53 green, 152 pink, 105 yellow, 116 orange

GAUGE

One triple-picot cluster (tp-cluster) = 3"/7.5 cm; 6 rows = 3 ½"/8.75 cm

CROCHET STITCHES USED

bead-picot (Wrap edging) — chain 1, pull up a bead, yarn over, pull up a loop, chi 1, slip st in back loop of first ch.

ch: chain

dc: double crochet

sc: single crochet

slip st: slip stitch

tp-cluster: triple picot cluster—work [sc, ch 7] 3 times, sc all in same stitch.

tr: treble crochet

tr4tog: treble crochet 4 together—leaving last loop of each tr on hook, work 2 tr in next sc and 2 tr in the following sc, yarn over, draw through all 5 loops on hook.

WRAP

Using larger hook and MC, chain 288.

Row 1 (RS): Work tp-cluster in twelfth ch from hook, * ch 4, skip 4 ch, dc into next ch +, ch 4, skip 4 ch, work tp-cluster in next ch; repeat from * across, ending last repeat at +, working final dc in last ch, turn—28 tp-clusters.

Row 2: Ch 1, sc in first st, * ch 1, sc into first arch of next tp-cluster, [ch 3, sc in next arch of same tp-cluster] twice, ch 1, skip 4 ch +, sc in next dc; repeat from * across, ending last repeat at +, sc in next ch (top of turning-ch), turn.

Row 3: Slip st (in each of next sc, ch-1, sc, ch-3, sc) to middle of first tp-cluster; ch 7 (counts as dc, ch 4), * skip [ch-3, sc, ch-1], work tp-cluster in next sc, ch 4, skip [ch-1, sc, ch-3], dc in next sc +, ch 4; repeat from * across, ending last repeat at +; leave remaining [ch-3, sc, ch-1, sc] unworked, turn—27 tp-clusters remain.

NOTE

Wrap is worked from upper
edge to point at lower edge.
Bead-picot stitch is worked along
edges of Wrap, then Flowers are
attached while working Picot
Bead edging around each Flower.

HELPFUL

When threading a large number
of beads onto a length of yarn,
wax the tip of the yarn with a little candle wax; shape to a point
before wax has fully cooled.

Rows 4 – 56: Repeat Rows 2 and 3, ending with Row 2—1 tp-cluster remains; do NOT turn after Row 56.

EDGING

Row 1: Working along row edges, ch 5, sc in final sc at end of last repeat of Row 2 (below); * ch 5, sc in final sc of next repeat of Row 2; repeat from * to corner; working across upper edge (in remaining loops of beginning chain), sc in each of next 2 ch, work 3 sc in next ch (upper corner), ** sc in each of next 4 ch, sc in ch beneath next tp-cluster, sc in next 4 ch, sc in chain beneath next dc; repeat from ** to ch beneath last dc of row, work 2 more sc in same dc (opposite upper corner); working along row edges, work 3 sc over post of same dc, sc in beginning sc of first repeat of Row 2 (above), *** ch 5, sc in beginning sc of next repeat of Row 2; repeat from *** to beginning of Row 56 (lower point). Fasten off.

Using MC, thread 57 beads onto yarn, alternating colors (yellow, orange, green, and pink), ending with yellow; join yarn with a slip st to upper left-hand corner.

Row 2: Ch 1, sc in same st, sc in each of the next 4 sc, * work bead-picot, sc in next ch-5 space, ch 4, sc in next sc *; repeat between *s along side edge to lower corner, work bead-picot, ch 4, skip [ch-1, sc, ch-3], sc in next sc, work bead-picot, sc in same sc, ch 4, skip [ch-3, sc, ch-1], sc in next sc; repeat between *s across to last 6 sts before next corner, work bead-picot, sc in each of next 5 sc, slip st in next sc. Fasten off.

FLOWERS

Make 41 in the following colorways: 6 using A as Color 1, C as Color 2 (A/C), 5 C/B, 6 B/A, 5 A/D, 4 C/A, 6 B/C, 5 A/B, and 4 D/A.

Using smaller hook and Color 1, leaving a 6"/15 cm tail for sewing, chain 4; join with a slip st to form a ring.

Round 1: Ch 1, work 9 sc in ring, join with a slip st in first sc—9 sc.

Round 2: Ch 1, work 2 sc in each sc around, join with a slip st in first sc—18 sc. Fasten off Color 1; join Color 2 with a sc in any sc.

Round 3: Ch 4, work [tr4tog (petal made), ch 4, sc in next sc, ch 4] 6 times, join with a slip st in first sc—6 petals. Fasten off.

Using Flower Placement Diagram as a guide, pin Flowers in place on Wrap.

EMBELLISHING

ATTACH FLOWERS

1. Pull 6"/15 cm tail from center of flower to right side. Thread 3 beads, matching petal color of Flower.

2. Thread yarn back through center hole of Flower to WS, being careful not to pull the beads through to the hole to the WS.

3. Sew Flower to the base of tp-cluster (see Diagram 2). Hint: Use a French knot to secure the yarn; pass the needle under the loop attaching the Flower to Wrap, pass needle through the loop just made, pull tight. Weave in end. Add beads to centers of remaining Flowers, attaching Flowers to Wrap as you go.

PICOT BEAD EDGING

This round adds a beaded edging to the Flowers and attaches the petals to the Wrap.

1. Thread Color 1 (center of Flower) with 6 beads, matching petal color of Flower.

2. Using smaller hook and Color 1 of Flower, working from the RS of Round 2, join yarn with a sc in the same sc of Round 2 as any sc on Round 3.

3. Working in front of Round 3, * ch 4, sc into top of petal, ch 1, slide down bead, yarn over, draw through loop on hook.

5. Return the dropped loop to hook and pull the loop through the stitch on the Wrap.

4. Remove loop from hook and pick up a stitch on the Wrap (below the bead), by inserting hook under the stitch.

6. Ch 1, insert hook in last sc made, yarn over, pull up a loop; push bead through the stitch to the RS; yarn over and draw through both loops on hook. Note: Working the sc in this manner will place the bead on the RS of the piece.

7. Ch 4, sc in same sc on Round 2 as next sc of Round 3 of flower; repeat from * of Step 3 around, end ch 4, join with a slip st to joining sc. Fasten off and weave in ends.

Repeat Picot Bead Edging on each Flower.

DIAGRAM 2

Beads

Attach Flower to base of Motif

FLOWER PLACEMENT DIAGRAM

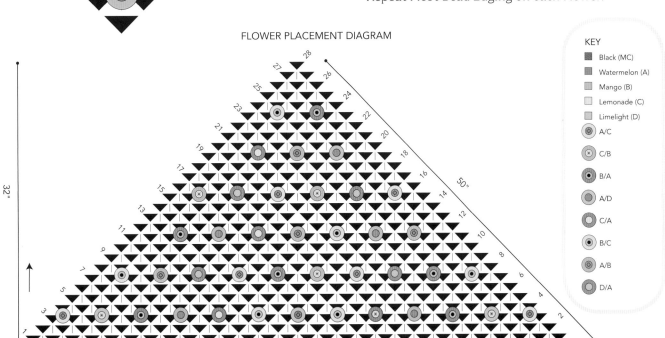

KEY

- ◼ Black (MC)
- ◼ Watermelon (A)
- ◼ Mango (B)
- ◻ Lemonade (C)
- ◻ Limelight (D)
- ◉ A/C
- ◉ C/B
- ◉ B/A
- ◉ A/D
- ◉ C/A
- ◉ B/C
- ◉ A/B
- ◉ D/A

32"

50"

84"

The Domino Effect

Think high contrasts…
yin yang…
domino games…
North Pole and the Black Sea…

Midnight Duster

DESIGNED BY LISA GONZALES

INTERMEDIATE

This easy-to-crochet duster is a modern take on a granny square theme. The center of each square is highlighted with a bead, making the duster simple but elegant. Dress it down for work or wear it over a frilly top for the evening.

SIZES

Small/Medium (Medium/Large, 1X/2X)

To Fit Bust 32–36 (38–42, 44–48)"/80–90 (95–105, 110–120) cm

FINISHED MEASUREMENTS

Bust 40 (50, 55)"/100 (125, 138) cm

Length 40"/101.5 cm, all sizes

YARN

Caron International's Simply Soft
(100% acrylic; 6 oz/170 g, 315 yds/288 m skein):

- #9727 Black, 9 (10, 12) skeins

CROCHET HOOK

One size US H-8 (5 mm), or size to obtain gauge

ADDITIONAL MATERIALS

- #16 tapestry needle
- 70 (86, 94) beads of choice (with a hole large for tapestry needle to fit through)
- Yarn needle

GAUGE

One Motif = 5"/12.5 cm square

In Mesh pattern (on sleeves),
5 sts and 5 rows = 4"/10 cm

CROCHET STITCHES USED

beginning cluster—ch 2 [yarn over, insert hook in same space, yarn over and pull up a loop, yarn over and draw through 2 loops on hook] twice, yarn over and pull through all 3 loops on hook.

ch: chain

cluster—[yarn over, insert hook in space indicated, yarn over and pull up a loop, yarn over and draw through 2 loops on hook] 3 times, yarn over and pull through all 4 loops on hook.

dc: double crochet

sc: single crochet

slip st: slip stitch

NOTES

1. Duster is designed to be loose fitting; fabric is very flexible, sizes are approximate.

2. Wear Duster overlapped in front, or open as shown in photo.

3. Motifs are worked, then joined into Strips and assembled for Back and Fronts.

4. Instructions given are for one length for all sizes; to shorten, work 1 or 2 fewer Motifs for each Strip.

5. Sleeves are worked upward from a 3-Motif strip, in Mesh pattern.

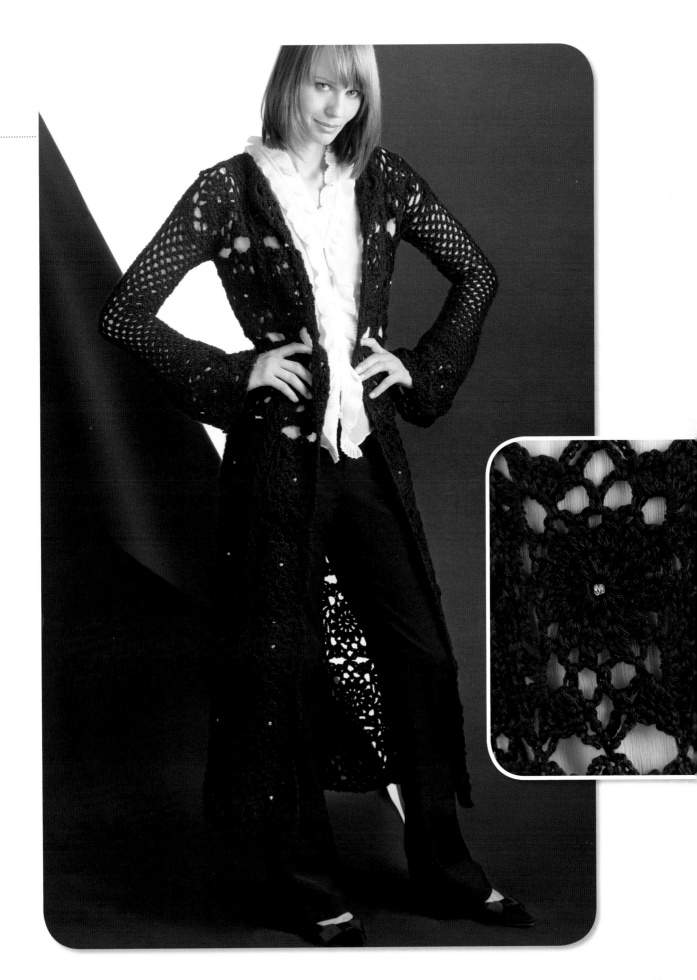

MOTIF [MAKE 70 (86, 94)]

Using larger hook, leaving a 6"/15 cm tail for attaching bead, chain 6; join with a slip st to form a ring, being careful not to twist chain.

Round 1: Ch 4 (counts as dc and ch 1), in the ring work [dc, ch 1] eleven times, join with a slip st in third ch of beginning ch-4—12 ch-1 spaces.

Round 2: Work a slip st and beginning cluster in next ch-1 space, ch 3 (counts as dc), work * cluster in next ch-1 space, ch 3; repeat from * around, join with a slip st in second ch of beginning cluster—12 clusters, 12 ch-3 spaces.

Round 3: Sc in next ch-3 space, ch 5, * sc in next ch-3 space, ch 5; repeat from * around, join with a slip st in first sc.

Round 4: Slip st in next ch-5 space, ch 3 (counts as dc), in same ch-5 space, work [dc, ch 1, 2 dc, ch 3, (2 dc, ch 1) twice] for first corner, sc in next ch-5 space, ch 5 (center space), sc in next ch-5 space, * in next ch-5 space, work [(ch 1, 2 dc) twice, ch 3, (2 dc, ch 1) twice] for corner, sc in next ch-5 space, ch 5 (center space), sc in next ch-5 space; repeat from * twice, ch 1, join with a slip st to top of beginning ch-3. Fasten off.

EMBELLISHING

ATTACH BEADS

Note that photos do not show Round 4.

1. After completing the motif, thread the tapestry needle with the 6"/15 cm tail.
2. Thread bead onto yarn.

3. Push the bead so it is close to the center ring of the Motif.
4. Use the yarn needle to attach the yarn end to the WS of the center ring. Knot securely and weave in end.

Tip: Put a very small drop of fabric glue on the knot to secure.

STRIPS [USING 8 MOTIFS PER STRIP, MAKE 8 (10, 11) STRIPS]

JOIN MOTIFS

Note: Edging is worked along one side of first Motif, then edging is worked along one side of second Motif, and AT THE SAME TIME, the 2 Motifs are joined together at each corner and in the center of the Motifs.

FIRST MOTIF

With RS facing, join yarn with a slip st in ch-3 corner space, * [(ch 2, slip st in next ch-1 space) twice, ch 5, slip st in center ch-5 space], ch 5; (slip st in ch-1 space, ch 2) twice, slip st in corner ch-3 space, ch 2, turn (WS of first Motif is now facing). Do NOT fasten off.

SECOND MOTIF

Place second Motif in front of first Motif, with WSs of the Motifs facing each other; slip st in the ch-3 corner space of second Motif, repeat from first bracket ([) under "First Motif" above through second bracket (]). Ch 1, slip st in the slip st worked in the center ch-5 space of First Motif, joining Motifs at center, ch 5; work to end as for First Motif, join last ch-2 worked with a slip st in ch-3 corner space of First Motif. Fasten off—2 Motifs joined.

Work 3 more sets of 2 Motifs—4 sets of 2 Motifs.

Join 2 sets together to make two 4-Motif strips; join 4-Motif strips to make 8-Motif Strip.

Continue in this manner until all 8-Motif Strips are completed.

JOIN 8-MOTIF STRIPS

Join 4 (4, 5) Strips for Back and 2 (3, 3) Strips for each Front as follows:

Hold 2 Strips together, with WS facing each other; join yarn with a sc in corner ch-3 space, working through both Strips; working along long edge through both Strips, * ch 3, slip st in next ch-space; repeat from * to end. Fasten off.

Continue in this manner until all Strips are joined for Back and Fronts.

Join side seams in the same manner, leaving 6 (6 ¾, 7 ½)"/15 (17, 19.5) cm open at upper edge for armhole.

Join shoulders, leaving 6 (6, 6 ½)"/15 (15, 16.5) cm free for Back neck; remainder of Fronts will fold forward.

SLEEVES (MAKE 2)

Join 3 Motifs to make a Strip.

With RS facing, join yarn with a slip st to corner ch-3 space of right-hand Motif.

Row 1: * Ch 3, sc in next ch-space; repeat from * twenty-two times evenly across, end by working last sc in corner ch-3 space, turn—23 ch-3 spaces (Mesh pattern).

Row 2: Decrease Row — Ch 3, skip first ch-3 space, sc in next ch-3 space, * ch 3, sc in next ch-3 space; repeat from * across, end sc in last ch-3 space, turn—22 ch-3 spaces remain.

Repeat Row 2 until 13 (15, 17) ch-3 spaces remain.

Next Row: * Ch 3, sc in next ch-3 space; repeat from * across; turn—13 (15, 17) ch-3 spaces.

Work 3 rows even.

Next Row: Increase Row — Ch 3, sc in first ch-3 space, ch 3, sc in same ch-3 space, * ch 3, sc in next ch-3 space; repeat from * across, turn—14 (16, 18) ch-3 spaces.

Work 4 rows even.

Repeat Increase Row—15 (17, 19) ch-3 spaces.

Work even until piece measures 19 (19 ½, 20)"/49 (50, 51) cm from beginning. Fasten off.

FINISHING

Join sleeves to armholes in the same manner as side seams, working evenly around armhole. Join Sleeve seams. Using yarn needle, weave in all ends.

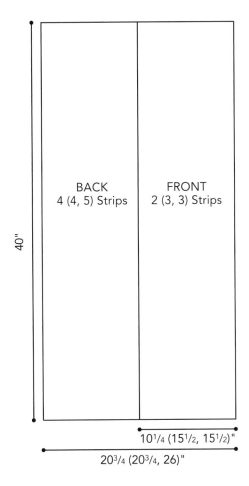

BACK
4 (4, 5) Strips

FRONT
2 (3, 3) Strips

40"

10¼ (15½, 15½)"

20¾ (20¾, 26)"

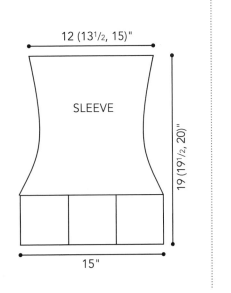

12 (13½, 15)"

SLEEVE

19 (19½, 20)"

15"

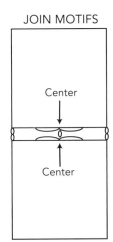

JOIN MOTIFS

Center

Center

Fly Away Purse

DESIGNED BY CARI CLEMENT

EASY

This chic purse is the perfect accessory for a night on the town. The feather fringe is a beautiful embellishment that makes the piece stand out.

ONE SIZE

FINISHED MEASUREMENTS

Width (lower edge) 10 ½"/26.5 cm; (upper edge) 7"/18 cm

Height 10 ½"/26.5 cm, excluding handles

Depth 2"/5 cm

YARN

Caron International's Simply Soft (100% acrylic; 6 oz/170 g, 315 yds/288 m skein):

- #9727 Black, 1 skein

CROCHET HOOK

One size US G-6 (4 mm), or size to obtain gauge

ADDITIONAL MATERIALS

Handles: One pair black plastic purse handles, with hooks at lower ends

Lining: Two sheets black plastic canvas, 10" x 12"/ 25 x 30.5 cm

Trim: ½ yard/45.5 cm each of the following:

- 4" – 5"/10 – 12.5 cm -wide feather trim;
- black and gray beaded trim;
- ½"/1.3 cm -wide black braid

Yarn needle

Chalk marker

Fabric glue

Scissors

GAUGE

Gauge is not critical for this project.

In half double crochet (hdc), 15 sts and 8 rows = 4"/10 cm

CROCHET STITCHES USED

ch: chain

hdc: half double crochet

sc: single crochet

slip st: slip stitch

NOTE

Purse is worked in 5 pieces; Back, Front, Bottom, and 2 Gussets. Back and Front of Purse are lined with plastic canvas to maintain its shape. Trim is applied after Purse is assembled.

BACK AND FRONT (BOTH ALIKE)

Chain 45.

Row 1: Hdc in third ch from hook and in each ch across, turn—43 hdc.

Row 2: Ch 2, hdc in each hdc across, turn—43 hdc.

SHAPE SIDES

Row 3: Ch 2, skip first hdc, hdc in each st across—42 hdc remain.

Repeat Row 3, decreasing 1 stitch every row until 25 hdc remain.

Work even, if necessary, until piece measures 10 ½"/26.5 cm from beginning. Fasten off.

GUSSETS (MAKE 2)

Chain 11.

Row 1: Hdc in third ch from hook and in each ch across, turn—9 hdc.

Row 2: Ch 2, hdc in each hdc across, turn.

Work even, repeating Row 2, until piece measures 3 ½"/9 cm from beginning.

SHAPE GUSSET

Increase Row: Ch 2, work 2 hdc in first st, hdc in each st across to last st, work 2 hdc in last st, turn—11 hdc.

Work even, repeating Row 2 until piece measures 7"/18 cm from beginning.

Repeat Increase Row—13 hdc.

Work even, repeating Row 2, until piece measures 10 ½"/26.5 cm from beginning. Fasten off.

BOTTOM

Chain 11.

Row 1: Hdc in third ch from hook and in each ch across, turn—9 hdc.

Row 2: Ch 2, hdc in each hdc across, turn.

Work even, repeating Row 2, until piece measures 10 ½"/26.5 cm from beginning. Fasten off.

FINISHING

Using yarn needle, weave in all ends.

LINING

Using Front, Back, and Bottom pieces as patterns, trace shapes onto plastic canvas, using a marker. Using scissors, cut out plastic canvas lining pieces. Using yarn needle threaded with a strand of yarn, whipstitch the lower edges of Front and Back lining pieces to the Bottom lining piece.

ASSEMBLE PURSE

With WS held together, join Front and Back pieces to Gussets by working 1 row of sc evenly along side edges through both pieces; join Bottom to Front, Back, and Gussets in the same manner.

HANDLE LOOPS
(MAKE 2 EACH ON BACK AND FRONT)

Right-hand side: With RS facing, join yarn with a slip st, one st in from right-hand seam on upper edge.

Row 1: Ch 1, * sc in next 3 sts, turn—3 sc.

Continuing on these 3 sts, repeat Row 1 until piece measures 1 ½"/3.5 cm from beginning, end with a WS row, turn.

Fold loop to WS; working through last row of Handle Loop and upper edge of Purse, slip st across, joining loop to WS of piece in the same sts worked on Row 1.

Left-hand side: With RS facing, join yarn with a slip st, 4 sts in from left-hand seam on upper edge. Work as for right-hand side.

Insert Lining into Purse: Whipstitch in place along upper edges of Back and Front. Insert the hook ends of the Purse Handles into the Handle Loops.

EMBELLISHING

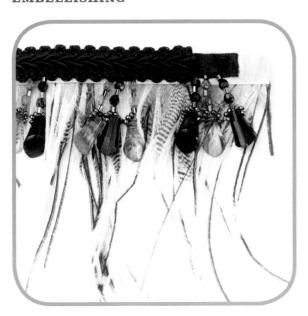

Attach trims: Note above photo shows each layer of trim in the order it is applied.

1. Cut feather trim to width of top edge of Purse.

2. Apply thin line of glue to back side of trim; adhere along top edge.

3. Cut beaded trim to width of top edge of Purse plus 1"/2.5 cm. Turn in ½"/1.3 cm on each end; glue wrong sides of each trim end together to secure.

4. Apply glue along top edge of feather trim; press beaded trim in place.

5. Cut braid trim to width of top edge of Purse plus 1"/2.5 cm. Turn in ½"/1.3 cm on each end; glue ends as for beaded trim.

6. Apply glue along top of beaded trim; press braid trim in place.

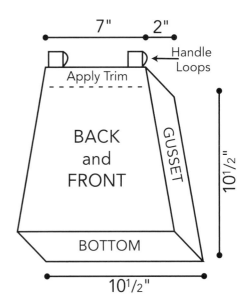

Elegant Squares Wrap

DESIGNED BY MARILYN LOSEE

INTERMEDIATE

This comfortable wrap is another take on granny squares, but this version is completely updated. It's sophisticated, sparkly, and so easy to make!

ONE SIZE

FINISHED MEASUREMENTS

Small Squares measures 14"/35.5 cm; Large Square measures 20"/51 cm

Wrap measures 48"/122 cm along one side, after assembly, excluding fringe

YARN

Caron International's Glimmer (85% acrylic, 15% polyester; 1.76 oz/50 g, 49 yds/45 m ball):

- #0019 Charcoal (A), 4 balls
- #0020 Black (B), 5 balls

Caron International's Simply Soft (100% acrylic; 6 oz/170 g, 315 yds/288 m skein):

- #9701 White (C), 1 skein, use double strand throughout

CROCHET HOOKS

One each size US K-10 ½ (6.5 mm) and L-11 (8 mm), or size to obtain gauge

ADDITIONAL MATERIALS

Yarn needle

3 yards/2.75 m beaded fringe

1 skein black embroidery floss

Sewing needle and black thread

6"/15 cm -wide piece of cardboard

Safety pin

GAUGE

Gauge is not critical for this project.

NOTE

Wrap is worked in 5 Squares, then joined (see Diagram); purchased beaded fringe is sewn to 2 long sides, Tassel is added to the neck edge of large Square and end folded down.

CROCHET STITCHES USED

ch: chain

ch-loop: chain loop—ch 10, slip st in top of dc just made.

dc: double crochet

joining-dc: joining double crochet—yarn over, insert hook in next dc, yarn over and pull up a loop, yarn over and draw through 2 loops on hook, insert hook in ch-loop, yarn over and draw through ch-loop and both loops on hook.

sc: single crochet

slip st: slip stitch

SMALL SQUARE (MAKE 4)

Note: RS is facing for all rounds.

Using larger hook and A, chain 4; join with a slip st to form a ring.

Round 1: Using A, ch 5 (counts as dc, ch 2), in the ring work 2 dc, work ch-loop, * dc, ch 2, 2 dc, work ch-loop; repeat from * twice, join with a slip st to third ch of beginning ch-5—4 ch-loops.

Round 2: Slip st in first ch-2 space, ch 7 (counts as first dc plus ch 4, now and throughout), work 2 dc in same space, dc in next 2 dc, work ch-loop, dc in next dc, * work [2 dc, ch 4, 2 dc] in next ch-2 space, dc in next 2 dc, work ch-loop, dc in next dc; repeat from * twice, dc in same space as first dc (beginning ch-7), join with a slip st to first dc (third ch of beginning ch-7)—28 dc, 4 ch-4 spaces.

Fasten off A; join double strand of C with a slip st in first ch-4 space.

Round 3: Using 2 strands of C held together, ch 7, work 2 dc in same space, dc in next 4 dc, work ch-loop, dc in next 3 dc, * work [2 dc, ch 4, 2 dc in next ch-4 space] for corner, dc in next 4 dc, work ch-loop, dc in next 3 dc; repeat from * twice, dc in same space as first dc, join with a slip st in first dc—44 dc.

Fasten off C; join A with a slip st in first ch-4 space.

Round 4: Using A, ch 7, work 2 dc in same space, dc in next 6 dc, work ch-loop, dc in each dc to corner, * work corner in next ch-4 space, dc in next 6 dc, work ch-loop, dc in each dc to corner; repeat from * twice, dc in same space as first dc, join with a slip st to first dc—60 dc.

Fasten off A; join B with a slip st in first ch-4 space.

Round 5: Using B, ch 7, work 2 dc in same space, dc in next 15 dc, * work [2 dc, ch 4, 2 dc] in next ch-4 space (corner), dc in next 15 dc; repeat from * twice, dc in same space as first dc, join with a slip st to first dc—76 dc.

Do NOT fasten off.

Transfer loop from hook to safety pin, to keep piece from unraveling while braiding ch-loops.

BRAID CHAIN-LOOPS

Working from center to outside edge, insert hook from front to back in first ch-loop (Round 1), * pull ch-loop on next round through ch-loop on hook; repeat from * twice, leaving last ch-loop free (to be joined on next round). Repeat braiding on remaining 3 sides.

Round 6: Continuing with B, return loop on safety pin to hook; slip st in first ch-4 space, ch 7, work 2 dc in same space, dc in next 9 dc, work joining-dc, dc in next 9 dc, * work [2 dc, ch 4, 2 dc] in next ch-4 space (corner), dc in |next 9 dc, work joining-dc, dc in next 9 dc; repeat from * twice, dc in same space as first dc, join with a slip st to first dc. Fasten off.

Using yarn needle, weave in ends.

LARGE SQUARE (MAKE 1)

Work Rounds 1—4 of Small Square—60 dc.

Round 5: Using B, work as for Round 4 of Small Square, working ch-loop above ch-loop of previous round—76 dc.

Round 6: Using A, repeat Round 5 of Large Square—92 dc.

Round 7: Using C, repeat Round 5 of Large Square—108 dc.

Round 8: Using A, work as Round 5 of Small Square, working dc in each dc between corners, work corners as established—124 dc.

Place last loop on safety pin. Braid ch-loops.

Round 9: Using B, work as Round 6 of Small Square, joining ch-loops with joining-dc.

Round 10: Using B, work as Round 5 of Small Square, working dc in each dc between corners, work corners as established. Fasten off. Weave in ends.

FINISHING

ASSEMBLY (SEE SCHEMATIC)

Using yarn needle and B, [join 2 Small Squares together] twice—2 strips of 2 Squares each.

Join one strip to each side of Large Square, as shown.

EDGING

Using smaller hook and B, join yarn with a slip st in any corner ch-space on outer edge; ch 1, work 2 sc in same space, work sc in each dc around, working 2 sc in corner loops where squares are joined and 4 sc in next 3 corners; in last corner (at beginning of round), work 2 sc in same space as beginning sc, join with a slip st to first st. Fasten off. Weave in end.

EMBELLISHING

ATTACH BEADED FRINGE

1. Pin beaded fringe to WS of lower edge of Wrap, turning in ends.

2. Sew to lower edge of Wrap using sewing thread.

MAKE TASSEL:

1. Wrap B around 6"/15 cm piece of cardboard to desired thickness.

2. Tie top of Tassel with length of embroidery floss.

3. Cut a 1-yard/92 cm length of B and thread through top of Tassel.

4. Trim bottom of Tassel evenly.

5. Wrap neck of Tassel with embroidery floss, leaving a 10"/25.5 cm length at one end, and secure. Pull long end of floss through top of Tassel. Tie securely at top of Tassel.

6. Thread short end through neck to skirt of Tassel.

7. With smaller hook and using floss end at top of Tassel, make a 2"/ 5 cm -long ch.

8. Fasten off, but do not cut yarn end.

9. Cut enough beaded fringe to encircle neck of Tassel and sew in place.

10. Using end of floss, sew Tassel securely to the point of large square, using Schematic as guide.

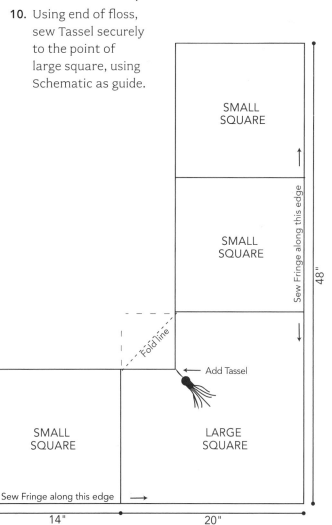

SMALL SQUARE

SMALL SQUARE

Sew Fringe along this edge

48"

Fold line

← Add Tassel

SMALL SQUARE

SMALL SQUARE

LARGE SQUARE

14"

Sew Fringe along this edge

14"

14"

20"

Cropped Vest

DESIGNED BY CARI CLEMENT

EASY

Tie an outfit together with this simple cropped vest. The beading
and detail around the trim is sure to spice up any look.

SIZES

X-Small (Small, Medium, Large, 1X, 2X)

FINISHED MEASUREMENTS

Bust 32 (36, 40, 44, 48, 52)"/81 (91.5, 101.5, 112, 122, 132) cm

Back Length (from shoulder) 13 (13, 13, 13 ½, 13 ½, 14)"/33 (33, 33, 34, 34, 35.5) cm

YARN

Caron International's Simply Soft Tweed (98% Acrylic, 2% Rayon; 3 oz/85 g, 150 yds, 137 m ball):

- #0002 Off White (MC), 2 (3, 3, 4) balls

Caron International's Simply Soft (100% acrylic; 6 oz/170 g, 315 yds/288 m skein):

- #9727 Black (CC), 1 skein

CROCHET HOOK

One size US H-8 (5 mm), or size to obtain gauge

GAUGE

In Pebble st, 16 sts and 15 rows = 4"/10 cm

ADDITIONAL MATERIALS

Yarn Needle

#16 tapestry needle

294 (312, 330, 362, 384, 406) large-hole 5/0 E seed beads, Matte Black (Miyuki)

CROCHET STITCHES USED

ch: chain

dc: double crochet

sc: single crochet

slip st: slip stitch

Bead Pebble Stitch (Edging)
Work as for Pebble st (below), sliding a bead down after dc and before sc; to turn corners, in corner work [3 sts in pattern in same st, adding 2 beads].

Decrease (dec)
Work 2 sts together in pattern to decrease 1 st, as follows:

- In pattern: [begin the next st in pattern, but to not complete it (leave 1 loop from the stitch on hook)] twice, yarn over, draw through all 3 loops on hook.
- For sc: insert hook into next st, yarn over and pull up a loop, leaving loop on hook.
- For dc: yarn over, insert hook in next st, yarn over and pull up a loop, yarn over and draw through 2 loops, leaving remaining loop on hook.

Pebble Stitch (multiple of 2 sts)

- ROW 1: Dc in third ch from hook, * sc in next st, dc in next st; repeat from * across, end dc in last ch, turn.
- ROW 2: Ch 2, * dc in next sc, sc in next dc, repeat from * across, end dc in top of beginning ch.
- Repeat Row 2 for Pebble st.

NOTES

1. Vest is worked in one piece to underarms, then Back and Fronts are worked separately to shoulders.

2. Beaded trim is worked after garment is assembled.

HELPFUL

Place a marker at the beginning of first row to indicate RS. Pebble stitch looks the same on both sides, therefore indications of RS and WS in instructions are to clarify instructions only.

VEST

Using MC, chain 130 (146, 162, 178, 194, 210).

Begin Pebble st, Row 1—128 (144, 160, 176, 192, 208) sts, counting beginning ch.

Work even in pattern, repeating Row 2, until piece measures 4 $^1/_2$"/11.5 cm from beginning (all sizes), end with a WS row; count in 33 (37, 41, 45, 49, 53) sts from each side, place a marker (pm) on these sts (center of underarm)—32 (36, 40, 44, 48, 52) sts each side for Fronts; 64 (72, 80, 88, 96, 104) sts for Back, including marked sts.

DIVIDING ROW

(RS) Work across 26 (30, 32, 34, 36, 38) sts in pattern for right Front, turn, leaving remaining sts unworked.

RIGHT FRONT

SHAPE ARMHOLE

(WS) Beginning this row, at armhole edge (beginning of WS rows, end of RS rows), dec 1 st every row 12 (12, 12, 14, 14, 14) times—14 (18, 20, 20, 22, 24) sts remain.

SHAPE NECK AND SHOULDER

(WS) Work across to last 3 (5, 7, 5, 7, 7) sts, dec across next 2 sts, turn, leaving remaining sts unworked—12 (14, 14, 16, 16, 18) sts remain.

(RS) Beginning this row, at neck edge (end of WS rows, beginning of RS rows), dec 1 st every row 10 times—2 (4, 4, 6, 6, 8) sts remain for shoulder.

Work even until armhole measures 8 $^1/_2$ (8 $^1/_2$, 8 $^1/_2$, 9, 9, 9 $^1/_2$)"/21.5 (21.5, 21.5, 23, 23, 24) cm (from dividing row. Fasten off.

BACK

With RS facing, beginning with marked st, skip 6 (6, 8, 8, 10, 12) sts to the left, counting underarm marked st; join yarn with a slip st in next st.

Ch 2, work in pattern across to 5 (5, 7, 7, 9, 11) sts before second marked st, turn, leaving remaining sts unworked—52 (60, 64, 72, 76, 80) sts for Back.

SHAPE ARMHOLES

(WS) Beginning this row, dec 1 st each side every row 12 (12, 12, 14, 14, 14) times—28 (36, 40, 44, 48, 52) sts remain.

Work even until armhole measures 6 (6, 6, 6 1/2, 6 1/2, 7)"/ 15 (15, 15, 16.5, 16.5, 18) cm from dividing row, end with a WS row.

SHAPE RIGHT SHOULDER

(RS) Continuing in pattern, work across 8 (10, 10, 12, 12, 14) sts, turn, leaving remaining sts unworked for neck and left shoulder.

(WS) Beginning this row, at neck edge dec 1 st every row 6 times—2 (4, 4, 6, 6, 8) sts remain for shoulder.

Work even until armhole measures 8 1/2 (8 1/2, 8 1/2, 9, 9, 9 1/2)"/21.5 (21.5, 21.5, 23, 23, 24) cm from dividing row. Fasten off.

SHAPE LEFT SHOULDER

With RS facing, skip center 12 (16, 20, 20, 24, 24) sts; join yarn with a slip st 8 (10, 10, 12, 12, 14) sts from left armhole edge, work to end.

(WS) Beginning this row, at neck edge dec 1 st every row 6 times—2 (4, 4, 6, 6, 8) sts remain for shoulder.

Work even until armhole measures 8 1/2 (8 1/2, 8 1/2, 9, 9, 9 1/2)"/21.5 (21.5, 21.5, 23, 23, 24) cm from dividing row. Fasten off.

LEFT FRONT

With RS facing, skip 6 sts after marked st, join yarn with a slip st in next st; ch 2, work in pattern to end.

SHAPE ARMHOLE

(WS) Beginning this row, at armhole edge (end of WS rows, beginning of RS rows), dec 1 st every row 12 (12, 12, 14, 14, 14) times—14 (18, 20, 20, 22, 24) sts remain.

SHAPE NECK AND SHOULDER

(RS) Work across to last 3 (5, 7, 5, 7, 7) sts, dec across next 2 sts, turn, leaving remaining sts unworked—12 (14, 14, 16, 16, 18) sts remain.

(WS) Beginning this row, at neck edge (end of RS rows, beginning of WS rows), dec 1 st every row ten times—2 (4, 4, 6, 6, 8) sts remain for shoulder.

Work even until armhole measures 8 1/2 (8 1/2, 8 1/2, 9, 9, 9 1/2)"/ 21.5 (21.5, 21.5, 23, 23, 24) cm from dividing row. Fasten off.

FINISHING

Sew shoulders seams.

Bead counts are what were used on sample garment, plus 10 to 12 extra; it's easier to have a few beads left on the yarn after finishing than to have to string additional beads to complete the edging; sample garment used approximately 14 beads per 6"/15 cm.

BEADED EDGING

1. Vest: Using tapestry needle, thread 164 (182, 196, 220, 238, 252) beads onto MC.
2. With WS facing, join yarn with a slip st to right Back neck edge at left shoulder seam.
3. Begin Bead Pebble st; work 1 row evenly across Back neck, along right Front neck shaping, down Front edge, across lower edge, up left Front and neck shaping (be sure to work the same number of beads on left Front as on right Front) to shoulder.
4. Armholes: Thread 70 (70, 72, 76, 78, 82) beads onto MC.
5. With WS facing, join yarn with a slip st to underarm at marker.
6. Begin Bead Pebble st; work 1 row evenly around armhole. Fasten off.
7. Count the number of beads used for armhole and thread an equal number for remaining armhole. Repeat Step 6 for remaining armhole.

EMBELLISHING

CROCHETED LOOP STITCH TRIM

1. Join CC to the WS of the center Back neck edge on the last row of the vest.

2. Insert the hook between the last row of the Vest and the beaded trim row from RS to WS; yarn over and pull loop through to RS and through loop on hook.

3. Skip 2 sts (1 bead); repeat Step 2.

4. Continue in this manner around Vest, taking care not to pull the loops too tightly.

5. Make three Lazy Daisy stitches on each corner of the lower Front and upper Front (see illustration on page 33), using photos as a guide.

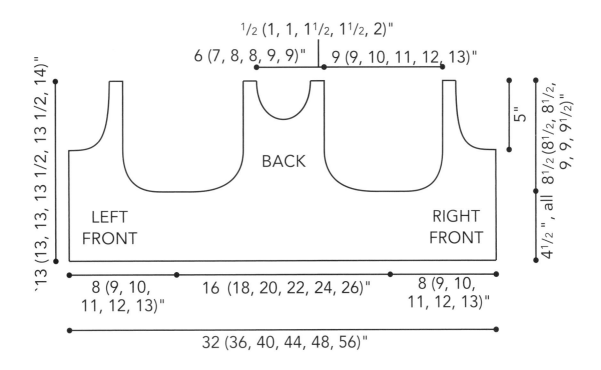

$^1/_2$ (1, 1, 1$^1/_2$, 1$^1/_2$, 2)"

6 (7, 8, 8, 9, 9)" 9 (9, 10, 11, 12, 13)"

13 (13, 13, 13 1/2, 13 1/2, 14)"

5"

8$^1/_2$ (8$^1/_2$, 8$^1/_2$, 9, 9, 9$^1/_2$)"

4$^1/_2$", all

BACK

LEFT FRONT

RIGHT FRONT

8 (9, 10, 11, 12, 13)"

16 (18, 20, 22, 24, 26)"

8 (9, 10, 11, 12, 13)"

32 (36, 40, 44, 48, 56)"

Out of Africa

Think desert shades…
colorful African fabrics…
equatorial jungles…
deep shadows and intense sunlight…

Sahara Shawl

DESIGNED BY MARGARET WILLSON

INTERMEDIATE

This amazing work of art is a definite show-stopper—you're bound to get noticed wherever you wear it. A variety of techniques (crochet stitches, embroidery stitches, and bead embellishments) are all showcased in this sophisticated shawl.

ONE SIZE

FINISHED MEASUREMENTS

Width 60"/152 cm, lower edge

Length 35"/89 cm

YARN

Caron International's Simply Soft
(100% acrylic; 6 oz/170 g, 315 yds/288 m skein):

- #9727 Black (MC), 2 skeins
- #9703 Bone (A), 2 skeins
- #9742 Grey Heather (B), 1 skein
- #9702 Off White (C), 1 skein

Caron International's Simply Soft Shadows
(100% acrylic; 3 oz/85 g, 150 yds/137 m ball):

- #0001 Pearl Frost (D), 2 balls
- #0008 Opal Twist (E), 1 ball

CROCHET HOOK

One size US I-9 (5.5 mm), or size to obtain gauge

ADDITIONAL MATERIALS

Yarn needle

Tapestry needle

Black beading thread

Beading needle (thin enough to fit through beads)

3 yards/2.75 m black flat braid or twill tape, ½"/1.3 cm wide

Straight pins

190 round wood bead, 6 mm, earthtone (Darice—Jewelry Designer #1905-08) — Bead-A

19 grams assorted bone beads, natural (The Beadery — elements #1433H) — Bead-B

23 grams assorted antiqued bone beads, black with white (The Beadery — elements #1438H) — Bead-C

75 wood beads, 8 mm — Bead-D

66 split cowrie shells — Bead-E

Split-ring stitch markers (optional)

GAUGE

In stitch pattern, Rows 1 – 12 form a triangle that measures 9" x 5"/ 23 cm x 12.5 cm

CROCHET STITCHES USED

bsc: bead single crochet (see page 12)

ch: chain

dc: double crochet

dc2-cluster: double crochet 2 together cluster— [yarn over, insert hook in next st and pull up a loop, yarn over and draw through 2 loops] twice, yarn over and draw through 3 loops on hook (one cluster made).

dc3-cluster: double crochet 3 together cluster— [yarn over, insert hook in next st and pull up a loop, yarn over and draw through 2 loops] 3 times, yarn over and draw through 4 loops on hook (one cluster made).

hdc: half double crochet

sc: single crochet

slip st: slip stitch

NOTES

1. Shawl is shaped by working increases both in the center st and at the beginning and end of rows, or at each of the 3 corners when rows are worked in the round (indicated as rounds).

2. Pay special attention to whether a row or round is indicated in the instructions, and whether it is right-side (RS) or wrong-side (WS) facing; do NOT turn unless indicated.

3. Beads are added on WS rows so that they will show on the RS.

4. It may be helpful to place a marker in center st when working increases, and move it up each row/round.

SHAWL

Note: All odd-numbered rows and rounds are RS until indicated otherwise.

Using tapestry needle and A, string 5 Bead-A on yarn, chain 6.

Row 1 (RS): Sc in second ch from hook, hdc in next ch, work 3 dc in next ch (2-sts increased — center), hdc in next ch, sc in last ch, turn—7 sts.

Row 2: Ch 1, [sc, bsc] in first st (increase), sc in next st, bsc in next st, work [sc, bsc, sc] in next st (center), bsc in next st, sc in next st, [bsc, sc] in last st (increase), turn—11 sts. Fasten off A; join C.

Row 3: Using C, ch 1, work 2 sc in first st (increase), sc in each st to center, work 3 sc in center st, sc in each st across to last st, work 2 sc in last st (increase), turn—15 sts.

Row 4: Ch 1, work 2 sc in first st, sc in each st to center, work 3 sc in center st, sc in each st across to last st, work 2 sc in last st, turn—19 sts. Fasten off C. Using E, string 13 Bead-B on yarn; join E.

Row 5: Using E, ch 3 (counts as dc), dc in first sc, dc in next 8 sts, work 5 dc in center st, dc in next 8 sts, work 2 dc in last st, turn— 25 sts.

Row 6 (WS): Ch 1, work [sc, bsc] in first st, * sc, bsc; repeat from * across next 10 sts, sc in next st ** [sc, bsc, sc] in center st; repeat from * to ** across next 11 sts, in last st work [bsc, sc], turn—29 sts. Fasten off E; join C.

Rows 7 and 8: Repeat Rows 3 and 4— 37 sts. Fasten off C. Using A, string 23 Bead-A on yarn; join A.

Row 9 (RS): Using A, ch 3 (counts as dc), dc in first sc, dc in each of next 17 sts, work 5 dc in center st, dc in next 17 sts, work 2 dc in last st, turn—43 sts.

Row 10: Ch 1, work [sc, bsc] in first st, * sc, bsc; repeat from * across next 20 sts **, [sc, bsc, sc] in center st; repeat from * to ** across next 20 sts, in last st work bsc, sc, turn—47 sts. Fasten off A; join C.

Rows 11 and 12: Repeat Rows 3 and 4—55 sts. Fasten off C; join MC, begin working in-the-round.

Round 13 (RS): Using MC, work 3 sc in first st (corner), sc in each st across to center, work 3 sc in center st; sc in each st across to last st (corner), work 3 sc in corner; working across top edge, work [1 sc in end of each sc row, 2 sc in end of each dc row and 1 sc in the remaining loop of each ch of beginning-ch (30 sc across top edge)], join with a slip st in beginning-sc, turn.

Round 14 (WS): Ch 1, * sc in each st around, working 3 sc in each corner and in center st, join with a slip st in beginning-sc, turn. Fasten off MC; join B.

Row 15 (RS): Using B, ch 3, dc in same st, dc in each of next 30 st, work 3 dc in center st, dc in each of next 30 st, work 2 dc in last st, turn.

Row 16: Ch 1, work 2 sc in first dc, sc in each st to center st, work 3 sc in center st, sc in each st across to last st, work 2 sc in last st, turn. Fasten off B. Using C, string 19 Bead-C on yarn; join C.

Row 17 (RS): Ch 1, work 2 sc in first st, sc in each st across to last st, working 3 sc in center st, work 2 sc in last st, turn.

Row 18: Ch 1, work 2 sc in first st, work [sc (bsc, sc in next 3 sts) 8 times, bsc, sc in next 2 sc] across to center st, work [sc, bsc, sc] in center st, sc in next 2 sts; repeat from [to] once, sc in next st, work 2 sc in last st, turn.

Row 19: Ch 1, sc in each st across, working 3 sc in center st, turn. Fasten off C; join B.

Row 20 (WS): Using B, ch 1, sc in each st across, working 3 sc in center st, turn.

Row 21: Ch 3, dc in first sc, dc in each sc across to last sc, working 3 dc in center st, work 2 dc in last st, turn. Fasten off B; join MC.

Row 22 (WS): Ch 3, dc in next 2 st, work [ch 3, skip 1 st, work dc3-cluster over next 3 sts] 10 times, ch 3, skip next st, work 3 dc in center st, ch 3, skip next st, work [dc3-cluster, ch 3, skip next st] 10 times, dc in next st, work 2 dc in last st, turn. Fasten off MC; join A.

Row 23 (RS): Using A, ch 1, sc in first 3 sts, [(working in front of ch-3 loop, work 3 dc in skipped st 1 row below, sc in top of next cluster) 10 times, work 3 dc in skipped st 1 row below] sc in next st, work 3 sc in center st, sc in next st; repeat from [to] once, sc in each of last 3 sts, turn.

Row 24: Ch 3, dc in first sc [(work 3dc-cluster, ch 3, skip next st) 11 times, work dc3 cluster] ch 7, skip center st; repeat from [to] once, work 2 dc in last st, turn. Fasten off A. Using MC, string 24 Bead-D on yarn; join MC.

Row 25 (RS): Using MC, ch 1, sc in next 2 st, sc in top of next cluster, [(working in front of ch-3 A-loop and around MC ch-3 loop (into the space) from 3 rows below, work 3 dc in skipped st 1 row below, sc in top of next cluster) 11 times], work 7 dc in skipped center st 1 row below, sc in top of next cluster; repeat from [to] once, work 2 sc in last st, turn.

Row 26: Ch 1, work 2 sc in first st, sc in next st, work [bsc, sc in next 3 sts] 12 times, work 3 sc in center st, [sc in next 3 sc, bsc] 12 times, sc in next st, work 2 sc in last st, turn. Fasten off MC; join C.

Row 27 (RS): Using C, ch 3, work 2 dc in same st, skip next st, sc in next st, [(skip next st, work 5 dc in next st working around ch-3 loop (into the space) that is at back of piece, skip next st, sc in next st) 12 times], work 5 dc in center st, sc in next st; repeat from [to] once, skip next st, work 3 dc in last st, turn. Fasten off C; join E.

Round 28 (WS): Using E, ch 1, sc in next 2 st, [(work dc3-cluster, sc in next 3 sts] 12 times, work dc3-cluster], sc in next st, work 3 sc in center st, sc in next st; repeat from [to] once, work dc3-cluster, sc in next st, work 3 sc in corner st, sc evenly across top edge as for Round 13, working 1 sc in each sc of Round 13, work 2 sc in corner, join, turn.

Round 29 (RS): Ch 1, then sc in each st around, working 3 sc in each corner and in center st, join. Fasten off E. Do NOT turn. Using C, string 64 Bead-A on yarn; join C.

Note: Even numbered rows and rounds are now RS until otherwise indicated.

Row 30 (RS): Using C, ch 3 (counts as dc), work 2 dc in same st, [(skip next st, work 2 dc in next st) 27 times, skip next st], work [2 dc, ch 3, 2 dc] in center st; repeat [to] once, work 3 dc in last st (upper right corner), turn.

Row 31: Ch 3 (counts as dc), work 2 dc in space between first and second dc, * work 2 dc in each space ** to center st, work [2 dc, ch 3, 2 dc] in center st; repeat from * to ** across to last 3-dc group, work 3 dc between second and third dc of last group, turn.

Row 32: Repeat Row 31.

Row 33: Ch 1, [sc, bsc] in first st, * work ch 2, skip 2, bsc in next space ** across to center st, [bsc, ch 3, bsc] in center st; repeat from * to **

across to last st, sc in last st, turn. Fasten off C; join A.

Row 34 (RS): Using A, ch 1, work 2 sc in first st, [work (3 sc in next ch-2 loop, 2 sc in next ch-2 loop) 15 times, 3 sc in next loop], work 5 sc in center st; repeat from [to] once, work 2 sc in last st, turn.

Rows 35 – 38: Ch 1, work 2 sc in first st, sc in each st across to last st, working, 3 sc in center st, work 2 sc in last st, turn.

Row 39 (WS): Ch 1, sc in first st, ch 2, sc in next st, [(ch 2, skip 3 sts, sc in next st, ch 2, skip 2 st, sc in next st) 12 times, ch 2, skip 3 st, sc in next st], ch 3, skip center st, sc in next st; repeat from [to] once, sc in next st, ch 2, sc in last st, turn. Fasten off A; join E.

Row 40 (RS): Using E, ch 3 (counts as dc), work 2 dc in first space, * work 3 dc in each ch-2 space ** across to center st, work [2 dc, ch 3, 2 dc] in center st; repeat from * to ** across to last ch-2 space, work 2 dc in ch-2 space, dc in last st, turn.

Row 41: Ch 3 (counts as dc), work 2 dc between first and second dc, * work 3 dc in each space ** across to center st, work [3 dc, ch 3, 3 dc] in center st, repeat from * to ** across to last 3-dc group, work 2 dc between second and third dc of last group, dc in last dc, turn.

Row 42: Repeat Row 41, turn. Fasten off E; join A.

Row 43 (WS): Using A, [sc, ch 1, sc] in first st, * ch 3, sc in next space **; repeat from * to center st, work [sc, ch 3, sc] in center st; repeat from * to ** across to last st, work sc, ch 1, sc] in last st, turn.

Row 44: Ch 1, sc in first st, work 2 sc in ch-1 space, * work 3 sc in each space** across to center st, work 5 sc in center st; repeat from * to ** across to last ch-1 space, work 2 sc in last space, sc in last st, turn.

Rows 45 – 47: Ch 1, work 2 sc in first st, sc in each st across to last st, working 3 sc in center st, work 2 sc in last st, turn.

Row 48 (RS): Work as Row 45, do NOT turn. Fasten off A; join MC, ready to work a RS row.

Row 49 (RS): Using MC, ch 1, work 2 sc in first st, * ch 2, sk 2, sc in next st; repeat from * across ** to center st, ch 3, skip corner st, sc in next st; repeat * to ** to last st, work 2 sc in last st, do NOT turn. Fasten off MC; join C, ready to work a RS row.

Row 50 (RS): Using C, ch 3, * work 3 dc in next st [skip ch-2 space, work 3 dc in next sc across] ** to center ch-3 space, work 3 dc in center ch-3 space; repeat from * to ** to last st, dc in last st, turn. Fasten off C; join MC.

Row 51 (WS): Using MC, ch 1, work 2 sc in first st, work [ch 2, sc in center dc of next 3-dc group across] to center st, ch 2, work [sc, ch 3, sc] in center st; repeat from [to] to last st, ch 2, work 2 sc in last st, turn.

Row 52 (RS): Ch 3, dc in first st, * skip next ch-2 space, work 3 dc in each sc across ** to center ch-3 space, work [3 dc, ch 3, 3 dc] in center ch-3 space; repeat from * to ** to last st, work 2 dc in last st, do NOT turn. Fasten off MC; join C, ready to work a RS row.

Rows 53 and 54: Using C; work as Rows 51 and 52. Fasten off C; join MC, ready to work a RS row.

Row 55 (RS): Using MC, work as Row 51, do NOT turn. Fasten off MC; join B, ready to work a RS row.

Row 56 (RS): Using B, ch 3, dc in same st, * work 3 dc in each ch-2 space across ** to center st, work [3 dc, ch 1, 3 dc] in center st; repeat from * to ** to last st, 2 dc in last st, turn. Fasten off B; join A.

Row 57 (WS): Using A, ch 1, work 2 sc in same st, sc in each st across to last st, working 3 sc in center ch-1 space, work 2 sc in last st, turn.

Row 58: Ch 3, dc in first sc, dc in each st across to last st, working 5 dc in center st, work 2 dc in last st, turn.

Row 59: Ch 1, work 2 sc in first st, sc in each st across, working 3 sc in center st, work 2 sc in last st, turn. Fasten off A; join D in first sc.

Row 60 (RS): Using D, ch 3, work 2 dc in same st, * (skip 2 sc, work 3 dc in next st) across ** to center st, skip 2 sc, work [3 dc, ch 3, 3 dc] in center st; repeat from * to ** to last 3 sts, skip 2 sc, work 3 dc in last st, turn.

Row 61: Ch 1, work 2 sc in first st, sc in each st across to last st, working 5 sc in center ch-3 space, work 2 sc in last st, turn.

Row 62: Ch 3, dc in first st, skip next st, work 3 dc in next st, * skip 2 sts, work [3 dc in next st, skip 2 sts] across ** to center st, work [3 dc, ch 3, 3 dc] in center st; repeat from * to ** across to last 2 sts, work 3 dc in next st, skip next st, work 2 dc in last st, turn.

Row 63: Repeat Row 61, turn.

Row 64: Ch 3, work 2 dc in first st, * skip 2 sts, work [3 dc in next st, skip 2 sts across ** to center st, work [3 dc, ch 3, 3 dc] in center st; repeat from * to ** to last st, work 3 dc in last st, turn.

Row 65: Repeat Row 61, turn. Fasten off D; join MC.

Row 66 (RS): Using MC, ch 3, work 2 dc in same st, * skip next st, work [2 dc in next st, skip next st] across ** to center st, work [2 dc, ch 3, 2 dc] in center st; repeat from * to ** to last st, work 3 dc in last st, turn. Fasten off MC; join A.

Row 67 (WS): Using A, ch 3, dc in same st * work 2 dc between the sts of each 2-dc group across ** to center ch-3 space, work [2 dc, ch 3, 2 dc] in space; repeat from * to ** across to last st, work 2 dc in last st, turn. Fasten off A; join MC in first st.

Row 68 (RS): Using MC, ch 3, dc between first and second st, ch 1, work dc2-cluster over next 2 spaces, ch 1, * work [dc2-cluster over previous and next space, ch 1] across ** to center space, working last dc in center ch-3 space, work [ch 1, dc] 3 times in center space, ch 1, work dc2-cluster over center space and next space, ch 1; repeat from * to ** to last 3 sts, work 2 dc between 2 sts, dc in last st, do NOT turn. Fasten off MC; join C, ready to work a RS row.

Row 69 (RS): Using C, sc in first st, work 2 sc between next 2 sts, * work 2 sc in each ch-1 space across ** to center st, work 3 sc in center dc; repeat from * to ** to last 3 sts, work 2 sc between next 2 sts, sc in last st, do NOT turn. Fasten off C; join B, ready to work a RS row.

Row 70 (RS): Using B, ch 3, work 2 dc between first and second sc, skip 2 sc, * work 2 dc in each space between 2-dc groups across ** to center st, skip 3 sc, work [2 dc, ch 3, 2 dc] in center sc, skip 3 sc; repeat from * to ** to last st, work 2 dc in last st, do NOT turn. Fasten off B; join MC, ready to work a RS row.

EDGING

Note: Work in rounds, join with a slip st in beginning sc at the end of each round.

Round 1 (RS): Using MC, work 3 sc in first st, * work 2 sc between sts of each 2-dc group across ** to center ch-3 space, work 5 sc in center space; repeat from * to ** to last st (corner), work 3 sc in corner, sc evenly across top edge as for Round 13, working 1 sc in each sc across sc of Round 28, join.

Rounds 2 – 4 (RS): Ch 1, then sc in each sc around, working 3 sc in center st and in each corner, join. Fasten off after Round 4.

EMBELLISHING

EMBROIDERY

1. Using tapestry needle and 2 strands B, work Cross stitch across Rows 17—19 between beads.

2. Using tapestry needle and 2 strands MC, work Fly stitch on Rows 35—37, working from each side toward center.

3. Using tapestry needle and 2 strands D, work Fly stitch on Rows 45—47, working from each side toward center.

4. Using tapestry needle and 1 strand MC, work Herringbone stitch on Rows 57—59, working from left to right to center, end at center; begin again, work to end.

BEADED FRINGE

PREPARE BRAID OR TWILL TAPE

1. Lay braid on flat surface.
2. Measure 1"/2.5 cm from end of braid, place marker.
3. Measure 1 ½"/3.5 cm from previous marker, place marker.
4. Repeat Step 3 for a total of 57 markers.
5. Leave 1"/2.5 cm of braid after last marker and cut away any excess braid.

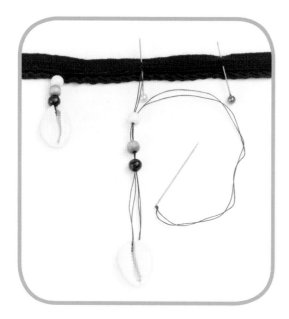

MAKE BEADED FRINGE ON BRAID

1. Thread beading needle.
2. Working from right to left, on WS of braid, backstitch to first marker.
3. Needle up at marker, thread 3 Bead-A (cream, tan, dark brown), thread cowrie shell from back to front, then thread needle up through first 3 beads.
4. Needle down at same marker, remove marker.
5. Backstitch on WS of braid to next marker.
6. Repeat Steps 3—5 across braid—57 Beaded Fringes.

ATTACH BEADED FRINGE TO SHAWL

1. With beaded edge of fringe against outside edge of Shawl, pin fringe to WS of edging, matching center dangle to center point and working toward each upper corner.
2. With WS facing, using tapestry needle and MC, baste fringe in place.

Right side of work

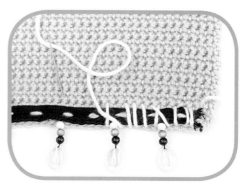

Wrong side of work

3. With RS facing, using tapestry needle and one strand of E, work Cross and brick stitch border over last 3 rows of edging, encasing Beaded Fringe (as follows):

Right-hand side: With RS facing, and straight edge of piece nearest, begin in corner with 3 straight stitches fanning out from same point. Work from right to left to upper corner.

Left-hand side: With RS facing, turn piece so that point of triangle is nearest and work from right to left to upper corner.

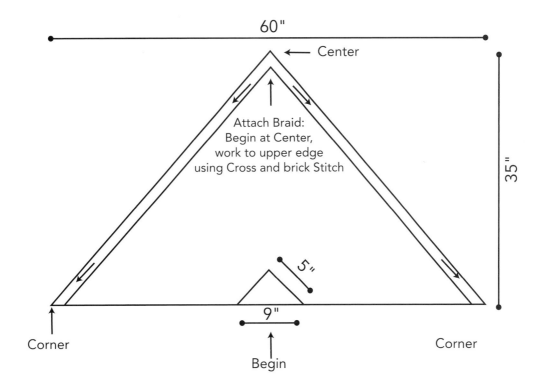

60"

Center

Attach Braid:
Begin at Center,
work to upper edge
using Cross and brick Stitch

35"

5"

9"

Corner

Corner

Begin

Herringbone stitch

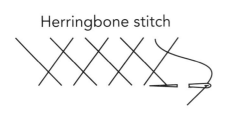

Fly stitch

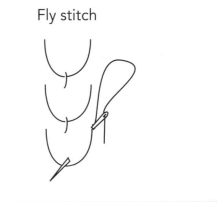

Cross and brick stitch

✕ | | |

Cross-stitch between beads

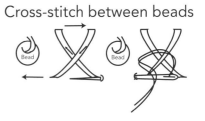

Desert Trader's Tote

DESIGNED BY CANDI JENSEN

EASY

This tote is a wonderful blend of sophistication and creativity, but is versatile enough to be paired with almost any outfit—whether you're out shopping or at the theater. This one-of-a-kind tote is not only functional, but a hip eye-catcher, too!

ONE SIZE

FINISHED MEASUREMENTS
14"/35 cm square

YARN
Caron International's Simply Soft
(100% acrylic; 6 oz/170 g, 315 yds/288 m skein):

- #9703 Bone (MC), 1 skein
- #9727 Black (A), 1 skein

CROCHET HOOK
One size US H-8 (5 mm), or size to obtain gauge

ADDITIONAL MATERIALS
- Yarn needle
- 1 package Foiled Oval Cheetah beads
  (The Beadery — Elements #1366H560)
- 2 packages cowrie shell beads, Natural
  (The Beadery — Elements #2050H)
- 1 42-oz package small oval gold beads
- 6 shell buttons
- ½ yard beaded fringe trim
- Blunt-end sewing needle
- Black sewing thread
- Beading needle (thin enough to fit through beads)

GAUGE
In half double crochet, 14 sts and 12 rows = 4"/10 cm

SPECIAL TECHNIQUE
Change color in last hdc: Work across to last st in current color; yo, insert hook in last st to be worked in current color and pull up a loop, drop current color, pick up next color, yo and draw through 3 loops on hook. Continue with new color.

CROCHET STITCHES USED
ch: chain

dc: double crochet

fpdc: front-post double crochet—(RS) yarn over, insert hook from right-hand side of stitch to WS of piece, return to RS of piece at left-hand side of stitch indicated, yarn over and pull up a loop, complete as dc.

hdc: half double crochet

sc: single crochet

slip st: slip stitch

BACK AND FRONT (BOTH ALIKE)
Using A, chain 11; join MC and chain 28; join another strand of A and chain 12.

Row 1: Using A, hdc in second ch from hook and in each of the next 10 ch, changing to MC in last st; using MC, hdc in next 28 ch, changing to A in last st; using A, hdc in last 11 ch, turn—50 hdc.

Row 2: Ch 2, hdc in each hdc across, changing colors as established, turn.

Work even, repeating Row 2, until piece measures 12"/30.5 cm from the beginning. Fasten off.

MEDALLIONS (MAKE 2)

Using A, chain 4; join with a slip st to form a ring.

Round 1: Ch 1, in center of ring work 12 sc, join with a slip st to first sc, turn—12 sc.

Round 2: Ch 3 (counts as dc), dc in first st, * dc in next st, work 2 dc in next st, repeat from * around, end dc in last st, turn.

Round 3: Ch 3 (counts as dc), dc in first st, * work [2 dc in next st, dc in next st] 5 times, work 2 dc in each of next 2 sts; repeat from * around. Fasten off. Using yarn needle, weave in ends.

EMBELLISHING

1. Using sewing needle and black thread, sew gold beads and shell beads in place on Medallions (see photo page 67).

2. Sew a shell button to each Medallion center.

3. Sew Medallions to Front (see photo page 67).

EMBROIDERY

String 16 Foiled Oval beads onto a strand of A (8 for each side of MC panel).

1. With WS of Front facing, beginning at lower edge, approximately 1 ½"/3.5 cm in from edge of MC panel, hold yarn to RS of piece; pull a loop from RS to WS through the Front and the loop on hook; * insert hook 1 ½"/3.5 cm above previous loop, slide a bead down, pull a loop through as for Step 1; repeat from * in a straight line to upper edge of Front (see photo).

2. Repeat 1 ½"/3.5 cm from opposite side edge of MC panel. Weave in ends.

FINISHING

With wrong sides facing, join Front to Back with a row of slip st, using A, along sides and lower edge.

EDGING

Work in rows; join at the end of each row before turning.

Row 1: With RS facing, using A, join yarn with a slip st to upper edge of Tote at side seam; ch 2, hdc in each hdc around, join with a slip st to first st, turn—100 hdc.

Row 2: Ch 2, hdc in each hdc around, changing to MC in last st, join with a slip st to first st, turn.

Row 3: Using MC, ch 2, * hdc in next 4 hdc, fpdc in next hdc of Round 1, repeat from * around, changing to A in last st, join with a slip st to first st, turn.

Rows 4 and 5: Using A, hdc in each st around, join with a slip to first st, turn. Fasten off. Weave in ends.

Cut 4 pieces of beaded fringe the width of side panels (A), plus 1"/2.5 cm. Fold under ½"/1.3 cm at each end; using sewing needle and thread, tack ends to WS, then sew fringe in place (see photo).

STRAPS (MAKE 2)

Using A, chain 80.

Row 1: Hdc in second ch from hook and in each ch across, turn—79 hdc.

Row 2: Ch 2, hdc in each hdc across.

Fasten off. Sew Straps to WS at upper edge of Tote (see photo). Sew a shell button on RS through both thicknesses to secure Handles to Tote.

Circular Yoke Blouse

DESIGNED BY GAYLE BUNN

INTERMEDIATE

Simply Soft yarn paired with the easy bead crochet stitch makes this project feel more like a knitted blouse than a sweater. This young and beautiful design is something you can wear to work, school, or play.

SIZES

Small (Medium, Large, Extra-Large)

FINISHED MEASUREMENTS

Bust 36 (40, 44, 48)"/91.5 (101.5, 112, 122) cm
Length 24 ½ (25, 25 ½, 26)"/62 (63.5, 64.5, 66) cm

YARN

Caron International's Simply Soft
(100% acrylic; 6 oz/170 g, 315 yds/288 m skein):

- #9703 Bone, 4 (4, 5, 5) skeins

CROCHET HOOK

One size US I-9 (5.5 mm), or size needed to obtain gauge.

ADDITIONAL MATERIALS

Stitch marker

Tapestry needle (thin enough to fit through beads)

54 (54, 62, 62) approximate 8 mm x 12 mm oval painted wood beads

GAUGE

In Cluster pattern, 6 clusters and 11 rounds = 4"/10 cm.

SPECIAL TERM

Cluster: Work 2 hdc in same space/st.

CROCHET STITCHES USED

bsc: bead single crochet (see page 12)

ch: chain

dc: double crochet

dc2tog: double crochet 2 together—[yarn over, insert hook in next dc and pull up a loop] twice, yarn over and draw through 2 loops] twice, yarn over and draw through 3 loops on hook.

hdc: half double crochet

sc: single crochet

sc2 tog: single crochet 2 together—insert hook in next st, yarn over and pull up a loop, yarn over and pull through 3 loops on hook.

slip st: slip stitch

BODY

Ch 126 (138, 150, 162) loosely; join with a slip st to first ch to form round, being careful not to twist chain.

CLUSTER PATTERN

Round 1: Ch 2 (counts as hdc), hdc in same ch as join (beginning cluster made), * skip next ch, work 2 hdc in next ch (cluster made); repeat from * around to last ch, skip last ch, join with a slip st to top of beginning ch-2—63 (69, 75, 81) clusters.

Round 2: Slip st in next hdc, slip st in space between beginning cluster and next cluster, ch 2, hdc in same space (beginning cluster made), * work cluster in next space between 2 clusters; repeat from * around; join with a slip st to top of beginning ch-2.

Repeat Round 2 for Cluster pattern until piece measures 5"/12.5 cm from beginning.

First Decrease Round: Slip st in next hdc, slip st in space between beginning cluster and next cluster, ch 2, hdc in same space, work [cluster in next space between 2 clusters] 18 (20, 22, 24) times, * [hdc in next space between 2 clusters] twice (cluster-dec made—counts as cluster) **, work [cluster in next space between 2 clusters] 19 (21, 23, 25) times; repeat from * once; then from * to ** once; join with a slip st to top of beginning ch-2—60 (66, 72, 78) clusters remain.

Work even in Cluster pattern until piece measures 9"/23 cm from beginning.

Second Decrease Round: Slip st in next hdc, slip st in space between beginning cluster and next cluster, ch 2, hdc in same space, work [cluster in next space between 2 clusters] 17 (19, 21, 23) times, * [hdc in next space between 2 clusters] twice **, work [cluster in next space between 2 clusters] 18 (20, 22, 24) times; repeat from * once; then from * to ** once; join with a slip st to top of beginning ch-2—57 (63, 69, 75) clusters remain.

Work even in Cluster pattern until piece measures 13"/33 cm from beginning.

Third Decrease Round: Slip st in next hdc, slip st in space between beginning cluster and next cluster, ch 2, hdc in same space, work [cluster in next space between 2 clusters] 16 (18, 20, 22) times, * [hdc in next space between 2 clusters] twice **, work [cluster in next space between 2 clusters] 17 (19, 21, 23) times; repeat from * once; then from * to ** once; join with a slip st to top of beginning ch-2—54 (60, 66, 72) clusters remain.

Work even in Cluster pattern until piece measures 15 (15, 15 $\frac{1}{2}$, 15 $\frac{1}{2}$)"/38 (38, 39.5, 39.5) cm from beginning.

LEFT FRONT

Row 1: Slip st in next hdc, slip st in space between beginning cluster and next cluster, ch 2, hdc in same space, work [cluster in next space between 2 clusters] 5 (6, 7, 8) times; leave remaining sts unworked; turn—6 (7, 8, 9) clusters for Left Front.

Decrease Row: Slip st in each of first 2 hdc, slip st in space between first 2 clusters, ch 2, hdc in same space (beginning cluster made), * work cluster in next space between 2 clusters; repeat from * to last cluster, leave last cluster unworked; turn—5 (6, 7, 8) clusters remain.

Repeat Decrease Row 3 (4, 5, 6) times— 2 clusters remain. Fasten off.

RIGHT FRONT

Row 1: With RS facing, skip next 12 (13, 14, 15) spaces between clusters; join yarn with slip st in next space, ch 2, hdc in same space (beginning cluster made), work [cluster in next space between 2 clusters] 5 (6, 7, 8) times, leave remaining sts unworked; turn—6 (7, 8, 9) clusters for Right Front. Complete as for Left Front.

RIGHT BACK

Row 1: With RS facing, skip next 3 spaces between clusters (underarm); join yarn with slip st in next space, ch 2, hdc in same space (beginning cluster made), work [cluster in next space between 2 clusters] 5 (6, 7, 8) times, leave remaining sts unworked; turn—6 (7, 8, 9) clusters for Right Back. Complete as for Left Front.

LEFT BACK

Row 1: With RS facing, skip next 12 (13, 14, 15) space between clusters; join yarn with slip st to next space, ch 2, hdc in same space (beginning cluster made), work [cluster in next space between 2 clusters] 5 (6, 7, 8) times, leave remaining sts unworked; turn—6 (7, 8, 9) clusters for Left Back. Complete as for Left Front.

SLEEVES (MAKE 2)

Ch 34 (34, 36, 36) loosely; join with a slip st to first ch to form round, being careful not to twist chain.

Round 1: Work as for Body—17 (17, 18, 18) clusters.

Continue in Cluster pattern until piece measures 2 $\frac{1}{2}$"/3.5 cm from beginning.

First Increase Round: Slip st in next hdc, slip st in space between beginning cluster and next cluster, ch 2, hdc in same space, * work cluster in next space between 2 clusters; repeat from * around to last cluster, hdc in each hdc of last cluster (cluster-inc made — counts as cluster); join with a slip st to top of beginning ch-2—18 (18, 19, 19) clusters. Place a marker (pm) on cluster-inc (underarm seam).

Work 9 rounds even in Cluster pattern.

Second Increase Round: Slip st in next hdc, slip st in space between beginning cluster and next cluster, ch 2, hdc in same space, * work cluster in next space between 2 clusters; repeat from * around to cluster above marked cluster-inc, hdc in each hdc of next cluster (cluster-inc made), ** work cluster in next space between 2 clusters; repeat from ** around; join with a slip st to top of beginning ch-2—19 (19, 20, 20) clusters. Move marker to cluster-inc.

Repeat last 10 rounds twice—21 (21, 22, 22) clusters.

Work even in Cluster pattern until sleeve measures 18"/46 cm from beginning. Fasten off.

SHAPE SLEEVE CAP

Row 1: Place marker on final row of sleeve at underarm seam. Leaving 3 spaces between clusters unworked at underarm, join yarn with slip st in next space between 2 clusters, ch 2, hdc in same space (beginning cluster made), work [cluster in next space between 2 clusters] 17 (17, 18, 18) times; leave remaining sts unworked, turn—18 (18, 19, 19) clusters remain.

Decrease Row: Slip st in each of first 2 hdc, slip st in space between first 2 clusters, ch 2, hdc in same space, * work cluster in next space between 2 clusters; repeat from * to last cluster, leave remaining cluster unworked; turn—17 (17, 18, 18) clusters remain.

Repeat Decrease Row 3 (4, 5, 6) times more— 14 (13, 13, 12) clusters remain. Fasten off.

YOKE

Sew Sleeves to Body at underarms.

Using tapestry needle, thread 28 (28, 32, 32) beads onto yarn.

Round 1: With RS facing, join yarn with slip st in right Back underarm seam; work 168 (168, 192, 192) sc evenly around yoke edge; join with a slip st to first sc.

Round 2: Ch 1, sc in same st as join, * ch 3, skip next 2 sc, sc in next sc; repeat from * around, end ch 3, skip last 2 sc; join with a slip st to first sc; turn—56 (56, 64, 64) ch-3 spaces.

Round 3 (WS): Slip st in each of next 2 ch, ch 1, sc in same ch-3 space, *ch 3, bsc in next ch-3 space, ch 3, sc in next ch-3 space; repeat from * around, ending with ch 3, bsc in next ch-3 space, ch 3; join with a slip st to first sc; turn—28 (28, 32, 32) bsc.

Round 4 (RS): Slip st in each of next 2 ch, ch 1, sc in same ch-3 space, *ch 3, sc in next ch-3 space, skip next sc and next ch-3 space, work 5 dc in next sc (fan made), skip next ch-3 space and next sc, sc in next ch-3 space; repeat from * around omitting sc at end of last repeat; join with a slip st to first sc—14 (14, 16, 16) 5-dc fans.

Round 5: Slip st in each of next 2 ch, ch 1, sc in same ch-3 space, * [dc in next dc, ch 1] 4 times, dc in next dc, sc in next ch-3 space; repeat from * around omitting sc at end of last repeat; join with a slip st to first sc.

Round 6: Slip st in next dc, ch 4 (counts as dc, ch 1), [dc in next dc, ch 1] 3 times, * dc2tog (last dc of fan and first dc of next fan) [ch 1, dc in next dc] 3 times, ch 1; repeat from * around, end dc in last dc; join with a slip st to third ch of ch 4 (counts as dc2tog)—56 (56, 64, 64) ch-1 spaces.

Round 7: Ch 1, sc in same st as join, *ch 3, skip next ch-1 space, sc in next ch-1 space, ch 3, sc in next ch-1 space, ch 3, skip next ch-1 space, sc in top of next dc2tog; repeat from * around omitting sc at end of last repeat; join with a slip st to first sc—42 (42, 48, 48) ch-3 spaces.

Round 8: Slip st in next ch-3 space, ch 3 (counts as dc), dc in same ch-3 space, * work 2 dc in next ch-3 space; repeat from * around; join with a slip st to top of beginning ch-3—84 (84, 96, 96) dc. Fasten off.

Using tapestry needle, thread 24 (24, 28, 28) beads onto yarn.

Round 9 (WS): With WS facing, join yarn with slip st in first dc, ch 1, sc in each of first 3 dc, * bsc in next dc, sc in each of next 6 dc; repeat from * around to last 4 (4, 2, 2) dc, bsc in next dc, sc in last 3 (3, 1, 1) dc; join with a slip st to first sc; turn—12 (12, 14, 14) bsc.

Round 10 (RS): Ch 1, sc in first sc, * ch 3, skip next 2 sc, sc in next sc; repeat from * around, end ch 3; join with a slip st to first sc—28 (28, 32, 32) ch-3 spaces.

Round 11: Work as Round 8—56 (56, 64, 64) dc. Do NOT fasten off.

Round 12: Slip st in next dc, slip st in space before next dc, ch 1, sc in same space, * ch 3, skip 2 dc, sc in space before next dc; repeat from * around, end ch 3; join with a slip st to first sc; turn—28 (28, 32, 32) ch-3 spaces.

Round 13 (WS): Slip st in each of next 2 ch, ch 1, sc in same ch-3 space, * ch 3, bsc in next ch-3 space, [ch 3, sc in next ch-3 space] 4 times; repeat from * 4 (4, 5, 5) times, end [ch 3, sc in next ch-3 space] 2 (2, 1, 1) time(s), ch 3; join with a slip st to first sc; turn—6 (6, 7, 7) bsc.

Round 14 (RS): Work as Round 8; turn—56 (56, 64, 64) dc. Do NOT fasten off.

Round 15 (WS): Slip st in next dc, slip st in space before next dc, ch 1, sc in same space, ch 3, skip 2 dc, bsc in space before next dc, * [ch 3, skip 2 dc, sc in space before next dc] 4 times, ch 3, skip 2 dc, bsc in space before next dc; repeat from * 4 times, end [ch 3, skip 2 dc, sc in space before next dc] 1 (1, 0, 0) time(s), ch 3; join with a slip st to first sc—6 (6, 7, 7) bsc. Fasten off.

FINISHING

TIE

Work a chain 58 (58, 60, 60)"/147 (147, 152, 152) cm long. Fasten off. Thread Tie through Round 13 of Yoke, beginning and ending at center Front. Attach one bead to each end of Tie.

CUFF EDGING

With RS facing, join yarn with slip st at under-arm of cuff edge in space between 2 clusters; ch 1, sc in same space, * ch 3, sc in next space between 2 clusters; repeat from * around ending with ch 3; join with a slip st to first sc. Fasten off.

BODY EDGING

Round 1: With RS facing, join yarn with slip st at center back of lower edge in space between 2 clusters, ch 1, sc in same space, * ch 3, sc in next space between 2 clusters; repeat from * around to last 1 (2, 1, 2) clusters, ch 3, skip 0 (1, 0, 1) cluster, sc between 2 hdc of next cluster, ch 3, skip remaining st(s); join with a slip st to first sc—64 (68, 76, 80) ch-3 spaces.

Round 2: Slip st in each of next 2 ch, ch 1, sc in same ch-3 space, * ch 3, sc in next ch-3 space, skip next sc and next ch-3 space, work 5 dc in next sc (fan made), skip next ch-3 space and next sc, sc in next ch-3 space; repeat from * around omitting sc at end of last repeat; join with a slip st to first sc—16 (17, 19, 20) 5-dc fans.

Round 3: Slip st in each of next 2 ch, ch 1, sc in same ch-3 space, * [dc in next dc, ch 1] 4 times, dc in next dc, sc in next ch-3 space; repeat from * around omitting sc at end of last repeat; join with a slip st to first sc.

Round 4: Slip st in next [dc, ch 1 and next dc], ch 4 (counts as dc, ch 1), [dc in next dc, ch 1] twice, * sc2tog (last dc of fan and first dc of next fan), [ch 1, dc in next dc] 3 times, ch 1; repeat from * around, end sc2tog, ch 1; join with slip st to third ch of beginning ch-4.

Round 5: Slip st in next ch-1 space, ch 1, sc in same ch-1 space, [ch 3, sc in next ch-1 space] twice, ch 3, * sc in next sc2tog, [ch 3, sc in next ch-1 space] 4 times, ch 3; repeat from * around, end sc in last sc2tog, ch 3, sc in next ch-1 space, ch 3; join with a slip st to first sc. Fasten off.

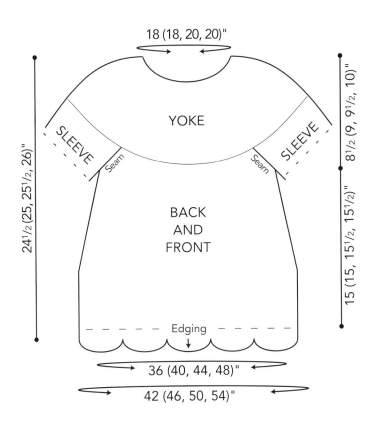

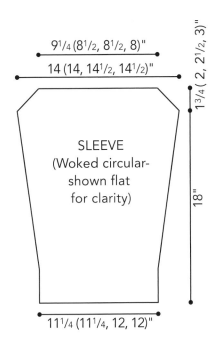

Hoop Earrings

DESIGNED BY NOREEN CRONE-FINDLAY

BEGINNER

There's no better way to learn bead crochet than by making these accessories. By splitting the four strands of Simply Soft Shadows into two strands, you can choose from a range of shadowed yarns to create your own unique earrings.

ONE SIZE

FINISHED MEASUREMENTS

2 ½"/6.5 cm in diameter

YARN

Caron International's Simply Soft Shadows (100% acrylic; 3 oz/85 g, 150 yds/137 m ball):

- #0004 Autumn, 1 ball

CROCHET HOOK

One size US C-2 (2.75 mm), or size to obtain gauge

ADDITIONAL MATERIALS

1 pair hoop earrings, 2 ¼"/ 5.5 cm in diameter

46 gold glass E beads, 4 mm

Beading needle (thin enough to fit through beads)

2 embroidery floss bobbins

Yarn needle

GAUGE

Gauge is not critical to this project.

CROCHET STITCHES USED

bss: bead slip stitch (see page 13)

ch: chain

dc: double crochet

slip st: slip stitch

NOTES

Earrings are worked using a 2-ply strand of yarn. Here is how to divide the strands.

1. Cut a 7-yard length of yarn and wind into a ball, leaving approximately 1 yard/92 cm free; secure ball with a yarn needle to hold the ball intact.

2. Separate the unsecured yarn end into two 2-ply strands, making sure there is one striped ply and one solid ply to each new pairing. Allow the ball to spin freely as it unwinds.

3. Wind 2-ply strand onto an embroidery floss bobbin.

4. Release another yard of yarn from the ball, secure it again with the yarn needle.

5. Repeat Steps 2–4 until the entire length of 4-ply yarn has been separated into two 2-ply strands.

EARRINGS (MAKE 2)

Using beading needle and 2-ply strand of yarn, thread 23 beads onto yarn; tie yarn end to earring hoop. Wrap yarn end around earring hoop and work over it while working Row 1.

Row 1: Insert hook into loop on earring and pull up a loop. Insert hook into center of earring hoop, yarn over and pull up a loop, take hook over earring hoop, yarn over and draw through both loops on hook (first chain made); ch 2, (counts as first dc), work 46 dc enclosing earring hoop.

Row 2: Flip the stitches through the earring hoop so they are standing vertically; working from back to front, bss 23 times.

FINISHING

Using beading needle threaded with tail, weave tail inside dc along outer edge of hoop. Trim ends.

Repeat for second earring, beginning at the opposite end of the earring hoop.

Kente Cloth Scarf

DESIGNED BY NOREEN CRONE-FINDLAY

INTERMEDIATE

This Tunisian crochet (a.k.a. Afghan stitch) scarf was inspired by traditional Kente cloth fabric. The colors in the scarf are mirrored by the delicate beaded fringe. Simply Soft makes this scarf super soft, and Noreen's experimentation with color makes this a bright, fun accessory to spice up any look.

ONE SIZE

FINISHED MEASUREMENTS

Width 6 ½"/16.5 cm

Length 65"/165 cm, excluding fringe

YARN

Caron International's Simply Soft
(100% acrylic; 6 oz/170 g, 315 yds/288 m skein):

- #9727 Black (A), 1 skein

Caron International's Simply Soft Brites
(100% acrylic; 6 oz/170 g, 315 yds/288 m skein):

- #9607 Limelight (B), 1 skein
- #9609 Berry Blue (C), 1 skein
- #9604 Watermelon (D), 1 skein
- #9605 Mango (E), 1 skein
- #9606 Lemonade (F), 1 skein

CROCHET HOOK

One Tunisian hook size US L-11 (8 mm), or size to obtain gauge

ADDITIONAL MATERIALS

Yarn needle

Tapestry needle

Beading needle (thin enough to go through beads)

Beading thread

4 large glass beads, ⅝"/1.5 cm, orange

24 glass beads, ⅝"/1.5 cm long, assorted greens

35 grams beads, ½"/1 cm, yellow mixed

35 grams beads, ½"/1 cm, blue mixed

2 packages beads (70 beads each) 6 mm, transparent blue

35-gram tube E seed beads, orange

35-gram tube E seed beads, assorted blues

35-gram tube E seed beads, assorted greens

35-gram tube E seed beads, black

Row counter (optional)

Ruler (for reading chart) (optional)

Beading tray (or muffin pan) for arranging beads (optional)

GAUGE

In Tunisian crochet, 15 sts and 9 rows = 4"/10 cm

STITCH USED

ch: chain

SPECIAL TECHNIQUE

Tunisian Crochet (Afghan stitch)

Each row of Tunisian crochet is worked in two steps after the Foundation Row.

Foundation Row

Chain the number of sts indicated in the instructions; skip first ch, * insert hook in next ch, yarn over and draw up a loop (2 loops on hook); repeat from * across, drawing up a loop in each ch. Complete Foundation Row by working Step 2. Repeat Steps 1 and 2 for remainder of piece.

STEP 1. With RS facing, working from right to left, pick up stitches for the row: Beginning in the second vertical bar of the previous row, * insert hook into the vertical bar of the previous row, yarn over and draw loop through the vertical bar (2 loops on hook); repeat from * across, drawing up a loop in each vertical bar.

STEP 2. Working from left to right, work off the stitches: yarn over and draw through first loop on hook, * yarn over and draw through 2 loops on hook; repeat from * across.

NOTES

1. Front of Scarf is worked first, from the Chart; the lining is picked up from the sts on the left-hand side of the scarf and worked across the width, then seamed. This means that it's not necessary to weave in yarn ends while working the Front.

2. Each square on the Chart represents one stitch.

3. When changing colors, always bring the new color under the working color to avoid holes from forming.

4. Bobbins are not recommended (see Helpful, below).

HELPFUL

1. When working from Chart, place a ruler on the Chart, covering the rows above the row that is being worked.

2. Due to the many color changes, it is recommended to cut yarn into 5-yard/4.5 m lengths; let them hang freely at the WS of the piece. The yarns will still tend to tangle, but the short lengths are easy to untangle.

FRONT

Foundation Row: Using A, chain 25. Follow instructions under Special Technique—24 sts. Work one row even. Begin Chart; work Rows 1—48 of Chart 3 times—145 rows total. Using A, work 1 row. Work 1 slip st in each st across, ending at upper left-hand corner of scarf.

LINING (REVERSE SIDE)

Continuing with A, ch 1; pick up 146 sts along side edge of Scarf; work sts off as Step 2—146 sts.

Stripe Sequence: Continuing to work in Tunisian crochet, work 2 rows using A, 2 rows F, 2 rows B, 2 rows D, 2 rows C, 2 rows E, 2 rows C, 2 rows D, 2 rows B, 2 rows F, 2 rows A.

Begin Stripe Sequence, counting pickup row as first row of A. Work even for 22 rows. Fasten off.

FINISHING

Fold Scarf in half lengthwise and stitch Lining to right-hand side of Front; stitch ends closed. If desired, steam Scarf, pressing flat with fingers; do not allow iron to touch Scarf. Using yarn needle, weave in ends from seaming.

EMBELLISHING

BEADED FRINGE

1. Sort beads into 24 groups, one for each 5"/12.5 cm fringe; begin by dividing larger beads, then filling in with the assorted colors of E beads.

2. Join the beading thread at one corner of the Scarf, anchoring securely.

3. Working across width of Scarf, using one group of beads at a time, thread the beads, ending with a large green bead and an E bead; working around the E bead, thread the needle up through the remaining beads to the edge of the Scarf.

4. Stitch through end of Scarf to anchor Fringe strand; stitch over one edge stitch of Scarf.

5. Working as for Steps 3 and 4, attach 12 Fringe strands across Scarf end. Fasten off securely.

6. Attach 12 Fringe strands to opposite end.

KENTE CLOTH CHART
24 sts; 48 row repeat

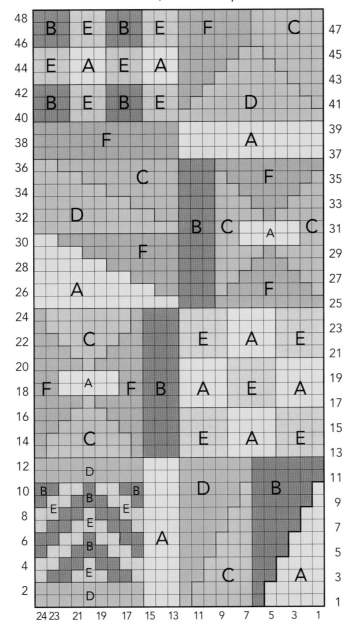

KEY

Lemonade (A)

Watermelon (B)

Limelight (C)

Mango (D)

Black (E)

Berry Blue (F)

Got the Blues

Think denims…

    basics blues accented with intense hues…

        applied embellishments…

            embroidered and trimmed jeans…

Medallions Belt

DESIGNED BY TREVA G. MCCAIN

EASY

Denim is a wonderful color to which you can add bright shades and sparkly trimmings, and the premade discs of plastic canvas act as a great armature or base to use in your embellishing projects. Play with the yarn, tassels, and beads to create your own signature belt.

SIZES

Small (Medium, Large)

FINISHED MEASUREMENTS

Length 33 (38, 43)", excluding Tassels

YARN

Caron International's Simply Soft
(100% acrylic; 6 oz/170 g, 315 yds/288 m skein):

- #9711 Dk. Country Blue (A), 1 skein
- #9710 Country Blue (B), 1 skein

Caron International's Simply Soft Brites
(100% acrylic; 6 oz/170 g, 315 yds/288 m skein):

- #9605 Mango (C), 1 skein
- #9604 Watermelon (D), 1 skein

CROCHET HOOK

One size US H-8 (5 mm), or size to obtain gauge

ADDITIONAL MATERIALS

Yarn needle

6—3" plastic canvas circles

30 g tube #3 seed rocaille glass beads, colors of mixed orange and hot pink, 1 tube

Larger blue beads for Tassels

Beading needle

2—2" D-rings

Large safety pin or sewing needle and thread (optional)

T-pins or straight pins (optional)

Cork board (optional)

GAUGE

Gauge is not critical for this project.

CROCHET STITCHES USED

ch: chain

dc: double crochet

dc3tog (cluster): double crochet 3 together—[yarn over, insert hook in next ch-2 space and pull up a loop, yarn over and draw through 2 loops] 3 times, yarn over and draw through 4 loops on hook.

fpsc: front-post single crochet—(RS) insert hook from left-hand side of stitch to WS of piece, return to RS at right-hand side of next dc from previous round (Note: This is the opposite direction from the normal working method for fpsc), yarn over and pull up loop, complete as sc.

sc: single crochet

slip st: slip stitch

SPECIAL TECHNIQUE

FIVE-STRAND BRAID

Note: The illustration on page 85 shows the path of each strand as it is braided; when repeating Steps 2 and 3, for each repeat the strand at the far left will be worked as for Strand 1 (Step 2), the strand at the far right will be worked as Strand 5 (Step 3).

1. Stitch or pin the ends of five strands together to secure, then pin strands to ironing board or cork board with T-pins.

2. Referring to the diagram, bring the left-hand strand (1) over the strand to its immediate right (2).

3. Weave the right-hand strand (5) over the strand to its immediate left (4), under the next strand (3) and over the next strand (1). Strand 2 is now at the far left, and Strand 4 at the far right.

4. Repeat Steps 2 and 3, always using the outer left-hand and right-hand strands.

NOTES

1. Depending on the hole size of the beads, it may be necessary to separate the yarn into 2-ply strands to be able to string on the beads. (See page 15.)

2. Make Belt longer or shorter by adjusting the number of beginning chains.

3. Flower Motifs are worked separately, applied to medallion bases, then attached to Braided Belt as desired.

BELT

Make 3 strands using A and 2 strands using B as follows:

Chain 276 (301, 326).

Row 1: Sc in the second ch from the hook and in each ch across, turn—275 (300, 325) sc.

Row 2: Ch 1, sc in each sc across. Fasten off.

Alternating colors (A, B, A, B, A), pin or baste strands together, then secure them to ironing board or a piece of cork board. Following instructions for 5-strand Braid technique, beginning at pinned end, braid cords until 18"/ 46 cm of cord remains at opposite end. Wrap a strand of A or B securely around strands to form a Tassel.

ATTACH D-RINGS

Using yarn needle and A, join the strands together close to the beginning of the Braid. Fold the ends through both D-rings; sew ends securely to WS. Using yarn needle, weave in ends.

FLOWERS

FLOWER MOTIF 1 (MAKE 2)

Using D, chain 4; join with a slip st to form a ring.

Round 1: Ch 5 (counts as dc, ch 2), working in the center of the ring, [dc, ch 2] 5 times; changing to C, join with a slip st in third ch of beginning ch-5—6 dc; 6 ch-2 spaces.

Round 2: Continuing with C, ch 4, * work cluster in ch-2 space of beginning ch of previous round, ch 4, work fpsc around next dc, ch 4; repeat from * 4 times, end cluster in next ch-2 space, ch 4, sc around first ch 2 of Round 1, join with a slip st in first ch of Rnd 2. Fasten off.

Using yarn needle, weave in ends. Using beading needle and yarn, attach 2 beads to each dc post of Round 1 (see photo above).

FLOWER MOTIF 2 (MAKE 2)

Using C, chain 4, join with a slip st to form a ring.

Round 1: Ch 1, work 12 sc into ring; do NOT cut C, changing to D, join with a slip st in first sc—12 sc.

Round 2: Using D, ch 1, [sc, ch 4, sc] in the front loop only of each sc of Round 1, join with a slip st in first sc of Round 2—12 small petals; cut D.

Round 3: Using C, working in back loops only of each sc of Round 1, ch 1, [sc, ch 7, sc] in back loop of each sc around, join with slip st in first sc of Round 3—12 large petals. Fasten off.

Using yarn needle, weave in ends. Using beading needle and yarn, attach 12 to 14 beads to the sc sts of Round 1 (see photo above).

FLOWER MOTIF 3 (MAKE 2)

Using C, chain 4, join with a slip st to form a ring.

Round 1: Ch 1, work 12 sc into ring; join with slip st to beginning sc—12 sc.

Round 2: Ch 5 (counts as dc, ch 2), dc in same space, skip 1 sc, [(dc, ch 2, dc) in next sc, skip 1 sc] 5 times; changing to D, join with a slip st in third ch of beginning ch-5—12 dc; 6 ch-2 spaces.

Round 3: Slip st in ch-2 space of beginning ch of Round 2, ch 3 (counts as dc), work 6 dc in same space, skip 1 dc, sc in space between skipped dc and next dc, skip 1 dc, * work 7 dc in next ch-2 space, skip 1 dc, sc in space between skipped dc and next dc, skip 1 dc; repeat from * around, join with a slip st to top of beg ch-3. Fasten off.

Using yarn needle, weave in ends. Using beading needle and yarn, attach beads in an X shape over the sc on Round 1; use 4 beads crossing from upper right to lower left, 5 beads crossing from upper left to lower right (see photo on preceding page).

MEDALLION BASES

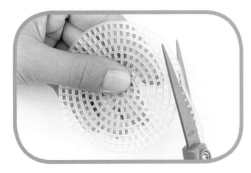

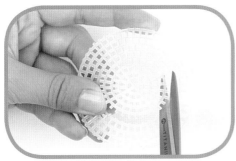

1. Using plastic canvas circles and sharp, pointed scissors, remove 1 outer section and 3 inner sections from 4 circles.
2. Remove 2 outer sections and 3 inner sections from 2 circles.

3. Using yarn needle and a double strand of A, cover circles with yarn, leaving last row at outer edge free (see photo above).

ATTACH FLOWERS TO MEDALLION BASES

1. Place Flower Motif on Medallion. Using yarn needle and a double strand of A, cover last row of canvas circle while attaching Flower to Medallion.
2. Attach Flower Motifs 2 and 3 to larger Medallions, Flower Motif 1 to smaller Medallions; when attaching Flower Motif 2, use 3 beads when securing outer petals to Medallion.

FINISHING

ASSEMBLY

Using yarn needle and A, attach assembled Medallions securely to the Braided Belt, evenly spaced. Note: Photo shows the smaller Medallions at each end.

TASSEL

Using beading needle and A or B, attach 3 larger beads to the end of each strand of Tassel (at opposite end from D-rings). If desired, attach 3 smaller beads, randomly spaced, up the length of each Tassel. Be creative!

5-STRAND BRAID

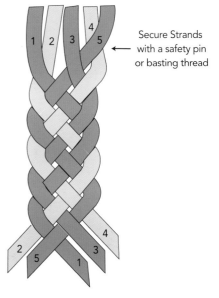

Secure Strands with a safety pin or basting thread

Denim Skirt

DESIGNED BY GAYLE BUNN

EASY

The classic, straight denim skirt was the inspiration for this more embellished version. Using different types of fringes and beads or, by changing the colors, you can create a whole wardrobe of Simply Soft skirts!

SIZES

Small (Medium, Large, Extra-Large)

FINISHED MEASUREMENTS

Hips 37 (39, 42, 45)"/ 94 (99, 106.5, 114) cm

Length 24 (24, 25, 25)"/ 61 (61, 63.5, 63.5) cm (including edging)

YARN

Caron International's Simply Soft
(100% acrylic; 6 oz/170 g, 315 yds/288 m skein):

- #9710 Country Blue, 3 (3, 4, 4) skeins

CROCHET HOOKS

Sizes US B-1 (2.25 mm) and US I-9 (5.5 mm),
or size to obtain gauge

GAUGE

In half double crochet, using larger hook,
12 sts and 8 rows = 4"/10 cm

ADDITIONAL MATERIALS

Stitch markers

Yarn needle

2 (2, 3, 4) spools metallic thread (5 yards/
  meters each)

Bead threader

33 (35, 38, 42) barrel beads

1 ¼ (1 ⅜, 1 ⅜, 1 ½) yards fringe, 2 ½" wide

Sewing needle and thread to match fringe trim
  and to match skirt

70 (74, 79, 84) square beads, 6 mm

Zipper, 7"/18 cm long

CROCHET STITCHES USED

bsc: bead single crochet (see page 12)

ch: chain

cl: cluster—work [2 dc, ch 1, 2 dc] in next stitch
  (or chain).

dc: double crochet

hdc: half double crochet

hdc2tog: half double crochet 2 together—yarn
  over, insert hook in next st, pull up a loop] twice,
  yarn over and pull through 5 loops on hook (1 st
  decreased).

sc: single crochet

slip st: slip stitch

NOTE

Turning chain (ch-2) does not count as a stitch.

BACK AND FRONT (BOTH ALIKE)

Beginning at lower edge, using larger hook, chain 65 (68, 73, 77).

Row 1 (RS): Hdc in third ch from hook and in each ch across, turn—63 (66, 71, 75) hdc.

Row 2: Ch 2, hdc in each hdc across, turn.

Repeat Row 2 until piece measures 3"/7.5 cm from beginning.

Decrease Row: Ch 2, hdc2tog, hdc in each hdc across to last 2 hdc, hdc2tog, turn—61, (64, 69, 73) hdc remain.

Work even for 3 rows.

Repeat last 4 rows 3 more times—55 (58, 63, 67) hdc remain.

Work even until piece measures 11 (11, 12, 12)"/27.5 (27.5, 30.5, 30.5) cm from beginning; place a marker (pm) each end of last row.

Next Row: Repeat Decrease Row, every other row until 41 (44, 49, 53) hdc remain for waist.

Work even until piece measures 7"/18 cm from markers. Fasten off.

BOTTOM EDGING

Using larger hook, chain 21.

Row 1 (RS): Dc in fourth ch from hook (counts as 2 dc), * skip next 3 ch, work cluster in next ch; repeat from * twice, skip next 3 ch, dc in each of last 2 ch, turn—2 dc at each end, 3 clusters.

Row 2: Ch 3 (counts as dc), dc in next dc, work [cluster in ch-1 space of next cluster] 3 times, dc in each of last 2 dc, turn.

Repeat Row 2 until piece, slightly stretched, measures 42 (44, 47, 50)"/107 (112, 118, 126) cm from beginning. Fasten off.

EMBELLISHING

BEADED ACCENT

1. Thread 17 (18, 19, 21) barrel beads onto 1 spool of metallic thread; thread 16 (17, 19, 20) barrel beads onto next spool(s) of metallic thread.

2. Using smaller hook, join metallic thread with a slip st in top corner of Bottom Edging.

3. Ch 1, sc in same space, work 3 sc across side of next row, * bsc in corner of next dc, work 6 sc across side of next 2 rows; repeat from * across, joining new spool(s) of thread as needed. Fasten off.

FRINGE

1. Using sewing needle and matching thread, sew square beads to top edge of fringe trim at ⅝"/1.6 cm intervals (see photo above).

2. Sew fringe trim across lower edge of Bottom Edging.

FINISHING

With RS facing, sew side seams of Back and Front, leave opening above markers on left side for zipper.

Using sewing needle and matching thread, sew zipper in place.

Sew seam of Bottom Edging; sew Bottom Edging to lower edge of Skirt, with seam at left side seam.

WAIST EDGING

With RS facing, using larger hook, join yarn with a slip st at upper edge beside zipper opening; slip st in each sc around waistline. Fasten off.

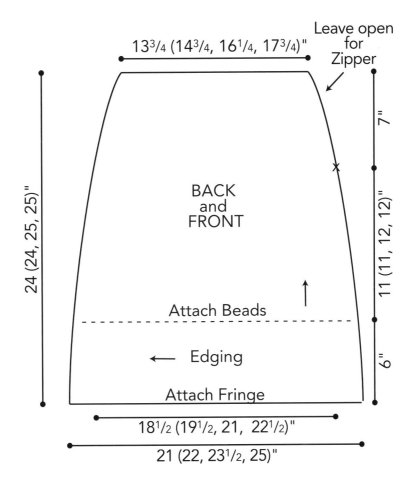

13¾ (14¾, 16¼, 17¾)"

Leave open for Zipper

24 (24, 25, 25)"

7"

BACK and FRONT

11 (11, 12, 12)"

Attach Beads

Edging

6"

Attach Fringe

18½ (19½, 21, 22½)"

21 (22, 23½, 25)"

Easy Beaded Camisole

DESIGNED BY GAYLE BUNN

This elegant camisole is a great design for your first embellishing project. It's versatile enough to wear by itself in the evening or over a shirt for a sophisticated look for day.

SIZES
Small (Medium, Large, Extra-Large)

FINISHED MEASUREMENTS
Bust 34 ½ (36 ¾, 40, 45 ¼)"/87.5 (93.5, 101.5, 115) cm

Length 18 ½ (18 ½, 19 ½, 20 ¼)"/46.5 (46.5, 49, 51) cm, including Straps

YARN
Caron International's Simply Soft
(100% acrylic; 6 oz/170 g, 315 yds/288 m skein):

- # 9709 Lt. Country Blue, 2 (2, 2, 2) balls

CROCHET HOOK
One size US I-9 (5.5 mm), or size to obtain gauge

GAUGE
In half double crochet, 15 sts and 9 rows = 4"/10 cm

ADDITIONAL MATERIALS
Beading needle (thin enough to fit through beads)

90 (92, 104, 110) beads, 8 mm, crystal

26 (26, 32, 34) beads, 8 mm, silver

Yarn needle

CROCHET STITCHES USED
bhdc: bead half double crochet—work as bsc, working hdc instead of sc.

bsc: bead single crochet (see page 12)

ch: chain

dc: double crochet

hdc: half double crochet

hdc2tog: half double crochet 2 together—yarn over, insert hook in next st, pull up a loop] twice, yarn over and pull through 5 loops on hook (1 st decreased).

sc: single crochet

slip st: slip stitch

NOTES
1. Chain-2 does not count as a hdc.
2. The beads are added in bead single crochet as the piece worked.

BACK
Thread 16 (16, 18, 20) crystal beads onto yarn. Chain 64 (68, 74, 84).

LOWER EDGING
Row 1 (RS): Sc in second ch from hook and in each ch across, turn—63 (67, 73, 83) sc.

Row 2: Ch 1, sc in first 1 (3, 2, 3) sc, * bsc in next st, sc in each of the next 3 sc; repeat from * until last 2 (0, 3, 0) sc, bsc 1 (0, 1, 0) time, sc in each of last 1 (0, 2, 0) sc, turn.

Row 3: Ch 2, hdc in each of the first 2 (2, 1, 2) sts, * ch 1, skip next sc, hdc in next st; repeat from * to last 1 (1, 0, 1) st, hdc in last 1 (1, 0, 1) st, turn.

Row 4: Ch 2, hdc in each of the first 2 (2, 1, 2) sts, * hdc in next ch-1 space, hdc in next hdc; repeat from * to last 1 (1, 0, 1) st, hdc in last 1 (1, 0, 1) st, turn.

SHAPE SIDES

(**Note:** Side shaping is written out below; it is also shown on Front Bead Placement Chart; work armhole and neck shaping as given for Back.)

Rows 1–4: Ch 2, hdc in each st across, turn.

Row 5: Decrease Row — Ch 2, hdc2tog (decrease), hdc in each hdc across to last 2 sts, hdc2tog over last 2 sts, turn—61 (65, 71, 81) sts remain.

Rows 6–8: Work even in hdc, (ch 2, hdc in each st across, turn).

Row 9: Repeat Decrease Row—59 (63, 69, 79) sts remain.

Rows 10–12: Work even in hdc.

Row 13: Increase Row — Ch 2, work 2 hdc in first st (increase), hdc in each hdc across to last st, work 2 hdc in last st, turn—61 (65, 71, 81) sts.

Rows 14–21: Repeat Rows 10 — 13 twice—65 (69, 75, 85) sts.

Rows 22–24: Work even in hdc.

SHAPE ARMHOLES

Row 25: Slip st in each of the first 7 (8, 9, 11) sts; ch 2, hdc in same space as last slip st, hdc in each hdc across to last 6 (7, 8, 10) sts, turn, leaving remaining sts unworked—53 (55, 59, 65) sts remain.

Row 26: Ch 2, hdc2tog, hdc in each st across to last 2 sts, hdc2tog over last 2 sts, turn—51 (53, 57, 63) sts remain.

Repeat last row 3 (3, 4, 6) times more—45 (47, 49, 51) sts remain.

SHAPE NECK

Next Row: Ch 2 [hdc2tog] twice, turn, leaving remaining sts unworked—2 sts remain.

Next Row: Ch 2, hdc2tog. Fasten off. With RS facing, skip center 37 (39, 41, 43) sts, join yarn with a slip st to next st; ch 2, hdc2tog over this st and next st, hdc2tog over last 2 sts, turn.

Next Row: Ch 2, hdc2tog. Fasten off.

FRONT

Thread beads onto yarn in the following sequence: 1 (1, 1, 2) silver beads, 7 (9, 9, 9) crystal beads, 8 (8, 8, 10) silver beads, [7 (7, 9, 9) crystal beads, 8 (8, 8, 10) silver beads] twice, and 16 (16, 18, 20) crystal beads.

EDGING

Work Rows 1—4 as for Back. Begin working from Front Bead Placement Chart, placing beads as indicated and working side shaping as for Back. Work Rows 1—24 of Chart.

SHAPE LEFT ARMHOLE AND NECK

Next Row: Slip st in each of the first 6 (7, 8, 10) sts; ch 2, hdc in same space as last slip st, hdc in each of the next 13 (13, 15, 19) hdc, turn, leaving remaining sts unworked—14 (14, 16, 20) sts.

SIZES SMALL, MEDIUM, AND LARGE ONLY

Next Row: Ch 2, hdc2tog, hdc in each of the next 4 (3, 3) hdc, bhdc, hdc in each st across to last 2 sts, hdc2tog over last 2 sts, turn—12 (12, 14) sts remain.

SIZE EXTRA-LARGE ONLY

Next Row: Ch 2, hdc2tog, hdc in each of the next 3 hdc, bhdc, hdc in each of the next 7 hdc, bead hdc, hdc in each hdc across to last 2 hdc, hdc2tog over last 2 hdc, turn—18 sts.

ALL SIZES

Next Row: Ch 2, hdc2tog, hdc in each st across to last 2 sts, hdc2tog over last 2 sts, turn—10 (10, 12, 16) sts remain. Repeat last row until 2 sts remain.

Next Row: Ch 2, hdc2tog. Fasten off.

SHAPE RIGHT ARMHOLE AND NECK

Thread 1 (1, 1, 2) silver beads onto yarn. With RS facing, skip center 25 (27, 27, 25) sts, join yarn with a slip st to next st; ch 2, hdc in same space as the slip st, hdc in each hdc across until last 6 (7, 8, 10) sts, turn, leaving remaining sts unworked—14 (14, 16, 20) sts.

Work as for left Armhole and Neck, reversing shaping.

FINISHING

NECK EDGING AND STRAPS

Thread 35 (36, 38, 40) crystal beads onto yarn. With RS facing, join yarn with a slip st at top corner of right Back neck edge. Ch 1, work 40 (42, 44, 48) sc evenly across Back neck edge to left side; ch 25 (25, 27, 27) for Strap, join with a slip st at top of left Front side; work 50 (52, 54, 58) sc evenly across Front neck edge to right side; ch 25 (25, 27, 27) for Strap, join with a slip st to first sc—140 sts, counting Strap chains.

Round 1: Ch 1, sc in each sc and ch around, join with a slip st to first sc.

Round 2: Ch 2, hdc in same space as joining; * ch 1, skip next sc, hdc in next sc; repeat from * around to last st, ch 1, skip last st, join with a slip st to first hdc, turn.

Round 3: Ch 1, sc in first hdc, sc in next ch-1 space, * bsc in next hdc, sc in next ch-1 space, sc in next hdc, sc in next ch-1 space; repeat from * around to last 2 sts, bsc in next hdc, sc in last ch-1 space, join with a slip st to first sc. Fasten off. Sew side seams.

ARMHOLE EDGING

With RS facing, join yarn with a slip st at side seam; work 1 round of sc evenly around armhole edge and sc in each remaining loop of chain along Strap, join with a slip st to first sc. Fasten off. Using yarn needle, weave in ends.

KEY

☐ Half double crochet

⊡ Silver Bead

⊙ Crystal Bead

Note: Do not add Bead shown in edge sts; work those beads only on larger sizes.

FRONT BEAD PLACEMENT CHART

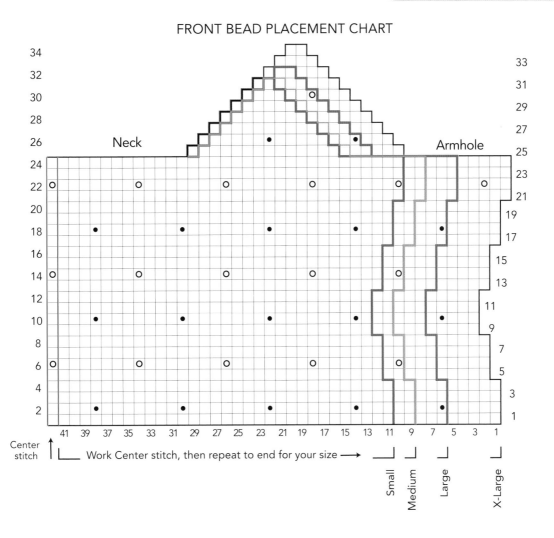

Color-Me-Blue Jacket

DESIGNED BY SUSAN SHILDMYER

EXPERIENCED

Crochet this lacy and delicate jacket to make a beautifully feminine garment. The floral embellishments and detailed trims make this jacket truly one of a kind.

SIZES

Small (Medium, Large, 1X, 2X)

FINISHED MEASUREMENTS

Bust 36 (40, 44, 48, 52)"/ 91.5 (101.5, 112, 122, 132) cm

Length 24 (25, 25 ½, 26 ¼, 27)"/ 61 (63.5, 64.5, 66.5, 68.5) cm, including edging

YARN

Caron International's Simply Soft (100% acrylic; 6 oz/170 g, 315 yds/288 m skein):

- #9710 Country Blue (MC), 3 (3, 4, 4, 4) skeins
- #9709 Lt. Country Blue (A), 2 (3, 3, 3, 4) skeins
- #9712 Soft Blue (B) 1 (1, 1, 1, 1) skeins

Caron International's Fabulous (100% nylon; 1.76 oz/50 g, 160 yds/146 m ball):

- #0010 Blue Lagoon (C), 1 (1, 1, 1, 1) ball, for embroidery

CROCHET HOOKS

One each size US 7 (4.5 mm) and US H-8 (5 mm), or size to obtain gauge

ADDITIONAL MATERIALS

Yarn needle

Two stitch markers

Embroidery needle and floss

Embellish Knit® Automatic Spool Knitter, (optional) OR 2 double-pointed knitting needles, for cording

GAUGE

In Stitch pattern, 17 sts and 13 rows = 4"/10 cm, using smaller hook and MC

CROCHET STITCHES USED

ch: chain

dc: double crochet

dc2tog: double crochet 2 together—[yarn over, insert hook in next st and pull up a loop, yarn over and draw through 2 loops] twice, yarn over and draw through 3 loops on hook.

hdc: half double crochet

sc: single crochet

slip st: slip stitch

Stitch Pattern (any number of sts) using MC
- ROW 1 (RS): Dc across all sts.
- ROW 2 (WS): Sc across all sts.
- Repeat Rows 1 and 2 for St pattern.

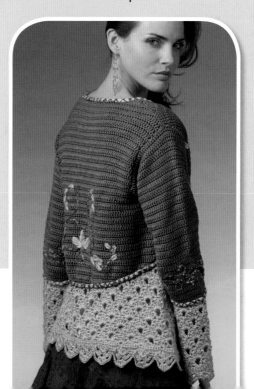

Lace Pattern (multiple of 8 + 1)

NOTE: Count sts on WS rows only; stitch count varies on RS rows.

ROW 1 (RS): Ch 1, sc in first sc, * ch 1, skip 3 sts, work [dc (ch 2, dc) 4 times] in next st, skip 3 sts, ch 1, sc in next sc; repeat from * across, turn.

ROW 2: Ch 4 (counts as dc, ch 1), skip [ch-1 space and dc], dc in next 2-ch space, ch 2, skip [dc, ch-2], sc in next dc, * ch 2, skip [ch-2, dc], dc in next ch-2 space, ch 1, skip next [dc, sc, dc], dc in next ch-2 space, ch 2, skip [dc, ch-2], sc in next dc; repeat from * across, end, ch 2, skip [ch-2, dc], dc in ch-2 space, ch 1, dc in beginning sc, turn.

ROW 3: Ch 5 (count as dc, ch 2), skip first dc, work [dc, ch 2, dc] in ch-1 space, ch 1, skip [dc, ch-2], sc in next sc, * ch 1, skip [ch-2, dc], work [dc (ch 2, dc) 4 times] in ch-1 space, ch 1, skip [dc, ch-2], sc in sc; repeat from * across, end ch 1, skip [ch-2, dc], work [dc, ch 2] twice in turning-ch, dc in third ch of turning-ch, turn.

DESIGNER'S NOTE: *[dc, ch 2] twice in turning ch, dc in third ch of turning ch* at end of this and subsequent rows means: *Work the sts from [to] into the loop of the turning-ch, then work the dc in the actual third ch of the turning-ch; this maintains a consistently straight edge to work from when finishing the Jacket.*

ROW 4: Ch 1, sc in first st, * ch 2, skip [ch-2, dc], dc in next ch-space, ch 1, skip [dc, sc, dc], dc in next ch-2 space, ch 2, skip [dc, ch-2], sc in next dc; repeat from * across, working final sc in third ch of turning-ch, turn.

ROW 5: Ch 1, * sc in first sc, ch 1, skip [ch-2, dc], work [dc (ch 2, dc) 4 times] in ch-1 space, ch 1, skip [dc, ch-2]; repeat from * across, end sc in last sc, turn.

Repeat Rows 2 – 5 for Lace pattern.

NOTES

1. Garment is worked in one piece from lower edge to armhole; then Fronts and Back are worked separately to shoulders.

2. While working Intarsia section, use larger hook for Lace pattern with A; smaller hook for Stitch pattern with MC.

JACKET

Using larger hook and A, chain 155 (171,187, 202, 219).

Setup Row: Sc in third ch from hook and in each ch across, turn—153 (169, 185, 201, 217) sts. Begin Lace pattern; work Rows 1 — 5 once, Rows 2 — 5 once, then Row 2 once—155 (171, 187, 202, 219) sts after Row 2; 153 (169, 185, 201, 217) sts after Row 4.

BEGIN INTARSIA

Row 11: Work in Lace pattern, repeating from * 8 (9, 10, 11, 12) times, dc in next sc; change to smaller hook and MC; work [2 dc in ch-2 space, dc in next dc, dc in ch-1 space, dc in next dc, 2 dc in ch-2 space, dc in next sc] twice, dc in next sc; change to larger hook and join a second ball of A; ch 2, skip [ch-2, dc], work [dc in (ch 2, dc) 4 times] in ch-1 space, ch 1, skip [dc, ch-2], sc in next sc; continuing in Lace pattern, work to end.

Row 12: Work in Lace pattern, repeating from * 8 (9, 10, 11, 12) times, ch 2, skip [ch-2, dc], dc in ch-2 space, ch 1; with MC; sc in each of next 17 dc; with A; ch 1, dc in next ch-2 space, ch 2, skip [dc, ch-2], sc in next dc; continuing in Lace pattern, repeat from * of Row 5 across, end as Row 5—155 (171, 187, 203, 219) sts.

Rows 13–22: Continue working Lace pattern as est, each side of MC section; work for your size as follows:

Small: Work Rows 13—16 twice, then Rows 19—22 twice.

Medium: Work Row 13—16 once, Rows 15—18 three times, then Rows 19—22 once.

Large: Work Rows 13—16 once, Rows 15—18 three times, then Rows 19—22 once.

1X: Work Rows 13—16 twice, Rows 15—18 twice, then Rows 19—22 once.

2X: Work Rows 13—16 three times, Rows 15—18 once, then Rows 19—22 once.

Row 13: Work in Lace pattern across to 20 sts before previous color change, end sc in next sc, ch 1, skip [ch-2, dc], work [(dc, ch 2) twice, dc] in ch-1 space; with MC, work [dc in next dc, 2 dc in ch-2 space, dc in next sc, 2 dc in ch-2 space, dc in next dc, dc in ch-1 space] twice, dc in each of the next 17 sc, work [dc in ch-1 space, dc in next dc, 2 dc in ch-2 space, dc in next sc, 2 dc in ch-2 space, dc in next dc] twice; with A, work [(dc, ch 2) twice, dc] in ch-1 space, ch 1; continue in Lace pattern to end.

Rows 14, 16, 18, and 20: Work in Lace pattern across to color change; with MC, sc in each dc across MC section; with A, work in Lace pattern to end—155 (171, 189, 203, 219) sts.

Row 15: Work in Lace pattern across to 8 sts before color change, end dc in next sc; with MC, work 2 dc in ch-2 space, dc in next dc, dc in ch-1 space, dc in next dc, 2 dc in ch-2 space, dc in next sc, dc in each sc across MC section, dc in ch-1 space, dc in next dc, work 2 dc in ch-2 space, dc in next sc, dc in ch-1 space, dc in next dc, 2 dc in ch-2 space; with A, dc in next sc, work in Lace pattern to end.

Row 17: Work in Lace pattern work across to 13 sts before color change, end sc in next sc, ch 1, skip [ch-2, dc], work [(dc, ch2) twice, dc] in ch-1 space; with MC, dc in next dc, work 2 dc in ch-2 space, dc in next sc, 2 dc in ch-2 space, dc in next dc, dc in ch-1 space, dc in each st across MC section, dc in ch-1 space, dc in next dc, work 2 dc in ch-2 space, dc in next sc, 2 dc in ch-2 space, dc in next dc; with A work [(dc, ch 2) twice, dc] in ch-1 space, ch 1, work in Lace pattern to end.

Row 19: Work in Lace pattern across to 4 sts before color change, end ch 1, skip [ch-2, dc], work [(dc, ch 2) twice, dc] in ch-1 space; with MC, dc in next dc, work 2 dc in ch-2 space, dc in next sc, dc in each st across MC section, dc in next sc, work 2 dc in ch-2 space, dc in next dc; with A, work [(dc, ch 2) twice, dc] in ch-1 space, work in Lace pattern to end.

Row 21: Ch 1, sc in first sc, skip [ch-2, dc], work [dc (ch 2, 2 dc) twice] in ch-1 space; with MC, dc in next dc, work 2 dc in ch-2 space, dc in next sc, dc in each st across MC section, dc in next sc, work 2 dc in ch-2 space, dc in next dc; with A, work [dc (ch 2, dc) twice] in ch-1 space, ch 1, skip [dc, ch-2], sc in last sc, turn.

Row 22: Repeat Row 14.

ALL SIZES

Row 23: Change to MC on all sts; ch 2, skip next dc, dc in ch-1 space, dc in next dc, work 2 dc in ch-2 space, dc in each st across MC section, dc in next sc, work 2 dc in ch-2 space, dc in next dc, dc in turning-ch, turn.

Row 24: Ch 1, work even in St pattern (sc in each st across), turn—155 (171, 189, 203, 219) sts.

SHAPE FRONT NECK

Row 1 (RS): Ch 2 (count as dc), at right Front neck edge, skip first sc, dc2tog across next 2 sts (decrease), dc in each sc across to last 3 sts, dc2tog across next 2 sts, dc in turning ch, turn—153 (169, 185, 201, 217) sts remain.

Row 2 (WS): Ch 1 (count as first st), skip first dc, sc in each dc across, turn.

Repeat Rows 1 and 2 once, then work even, if necessary, until piece measures 13 ½ (14, 14, 14 ½, 14 ½)"/34.5 (36.5, 36.5, 37, 37) cm from beginning, end with a WS row—151 (167, 183, 199, 215) sts remain.

DIVIDING ROW

Row 1 (RS): At right Front neck edge, ch 2, skip first sc, dc2tog, dc across next 26 (30, 35, 37, 39) sts; at armhole edge, dc2tog, place marker (pm), turn, leave remaining sts unworked—29 (33, 38, 40, 42) sts for right Front.

Row 2 (WS): Ch 1, skip first dc, work even in sc, turn.

Rows 3–4 (4, 6, 6, 6): Repeat Rows 1 and 2—27 (31, 34, 36, 38) sts remain.

Next Row (RS): Ch 2, skip first sc, dc2tog, dc to end—26 (30, 33, 35, 37) sts remain.

Continue in pattern; at neck edge, dec 1 st every other row 10 (11, 11, 10, 10) times—16 (19, 22, 25, 27) sts remain for shoulder.

Work even until armhole measures 7 ½ (8, 8 ½, 8 ¾, 9)"/19.5 (20.5, 21.5, 22, 23) cm from marker, end with a WS row.

SHAPE SHOULDER

Row 1 (RS): Ch 2, skip first sc, dc in next 7 (10, 12, 14, 16) sc, hdc in next st, sc in next st, turn, leaving remaining sts unworked—10 (13, 15, 17, 19) sts.

Row 2 (WS): Slip st in first st, sc in each st across to last st, slip st in last st, turn—9 (12, 14, 16, 18) sts remain.

Row 3: Ch 2 (counts as dc), skip first sc, dc in next 2 (4, 5, 5, 6) sts, hdc in next st, sc in next st, leave remaining sts unworked. Fasten off.

BACK

With RS facing, beginning at underarm marker, skip 14 (16, 16, 18, 20) sts; join MC with a slip st in next st.

Row 1 (RS): Ch 2, dc2tog (1 st decrease), dc in each of the next 51 (57, 63, 71, 79) sts, dc2tog, dc in next st; pm, turn, leaving remaining sts unworked—55 (61, 67, 75, 83) sts.

Row 2 (WS): Ch 1, skip first dc, work even in sc, turn.

Rows 3–4 (4, 6, 6, 6): Repeat Rows 1 and 2—53 (59, 63, 71, 77) sts.

Work even in established pattern until Back measures the same as right Front to shoulder shaping, end with a WS row.

SHAPE SHOULDERS AND NECK

(RS): Slip st in next 5 (6, 6, 8, 8) sts, [sc, hdc] across next 2 sts, dc in each sc across to last 7 (8, 8, 10, 10) sts, hdc, sc, turn, leaving remaining sts unworked—43 (47, 51, 55, 61) sts remain.

(WS): Slip st in first st, sc in each st across to last st, slip st in last st, turn — 41(45, 49, 53, 59) sts remain.

(RS): Slip st in next 5 (5, 6, 8, 9) sts, [sc, hdc] across next 2 sts, dc in next 2 (5, 6, 6, 7) sts. Fasten off. Skip center 27 (28, 29, 29, 32) sts for Back neck. Join MC with a slip st in next st; ch 2, dc in the next 2 (4, 5, 5, 6) sts, [hdc, sc] across next 2 sts, leave remaining sts unworked. Fasten off.

LEFT FRONT

With RS facing, beginning at marker, skip 14 (16, 16, 18, 20) sts; join MC with a slip st in next st. Work as for right Front, reversing all shaping

SLEEVES

Using A and larger hook, ch 50 (50, 58, 58, 58), turn.

Row 1: Sc in second ch from hook and in each sc across, turn—49 (49, 57, 57, 57) sts.

(RS): Begin Lace pattern; work even until piece measures 6 ½ (7, 7, 7 ½, 7 ½)"/16.5 (18, 18, 19.5, 19.5) cm from beginning, end with a WS row. Change to MC and smaller hook.

Note: Work next row as Row 1a or Row 1b, depending on last Row of Lace pattern worked, then continue as indicated.

IF LAST ROW WAS ROW 2 OF LACE PATTERN:

Row 1a (RS): Ch 2, dc in ch-1 space,* dc in next dc, work 2 dc in ch-2 space, dc in next st, work 2 dc in ch-2 space, dc in next 2 sts; repeat from * to end, working last dc in the fourth ch of the turning ch, turn—49 (49, 57, 57, 57) sts.

IF LAST ROW WAS ROW 4 OF LACE PATTERN:

Row 1b (RS): Ch 2, * work 2 dc in ch-2 space, dc in next dc, dc in ch-1 space, dc in next dc, work 2 dc in ch-2 space, dc in next st; repeat from * to end, turn—49 (49, 57, 57, 57) sts.

Row 2 (WS): Ch 1, work even in sc, turn.

SHAPE SLEEVE

Row 3 (RS): Work 2 dc in first sc (increase), dc in each sc across to last sc, work 2 dc in last sc (increase), turn. Continuing in pattern, work 1 row even.

Repeat last 2 rows 7 (9, 7, 8, 9) times, increasing 1 st each side every other row—65 (69, 73, 75, 77) sts.

Work even in pattern until MC section of piece measures 14 (14, 14 ½, 14 ½)"/36.5 (36.5, 37, 37, 38) cm from beginning, end with a WS row.

SHAPE CAP

(RS): Dec 1 st each side every other row 2 (2, 3, 3, 4) times—61 (65, 67, 69, 69) sts remain. Fasten off.

FINISHING

Sew shoulder seams.

LOWER EDGING

Note: Row 1 is worked in the remaining loops of beginning-ch.

Row 1 (RS): Join A with a slip st in first ch; ch 1, sc in next 3 ch, * ch 2, skip next ch, work [2 dc, ch 2] twice in next ch, skip 1 ch, sc in next 5 ch; repeat from * across, turn.

Row 2: Ch 1, sc in next 4 sc, skip next st, * ch 3, skip ch-2 space, work [2 dc, ch 2, 2 dc] in next ch-2 space, ch 3, skip [next ch-2 space and sc], sc in next 3 sc, skip 1; repeat from * across, end last repeat skip [next ch-2 space and sc], sc in next 2 sc, sc in turning ch, turn.

Row 3: Ch 1, first 2 sc, skip next sc, * ch 5, skip ch-3 space, work [2 dc, ch 2, 2 dc] in next ch-2

space, ch 5, skip [next ch-3 space and sc], sc in next sc; repeat from * across to last 2 sts, sc in last 2 sc.

Sizes Small, Medium, Large, and 1X — Fasten off.

SIZE 2X ONLY:

Row 4: Ch 1, sc in first st, skip next sc * ch 7, skip ch-5 space, work [2 dc, ch 2, 2 dc] in next ch-2 space, ch 7, skip ch-5 space, sc in next sc; repeat from * across to last 2 sts, skip next sc, sc in last sc. Fasten off.

NECK EDGING

With RS facing, beginning at right Front at beginning of neck shaping, using smaller hook and MC, join yarn with a slip to first st; ch 1, work 1 row sc evenly around neck shaping, ending at left Front.

LOWER FRONT EDGING

With RS facing, working along lace sections of each Front, using larger hook and A, join yarn and work as for neck edging, working 1 row sc evenly along Front edges. Fasten off.

SLEEVE EDGING

Work same as for Lower Edging along each Sleeve.

EMBELLISHING

MAKE CORDING

Note: Make each length of cord slightly longer than actual garment measurement, bind off loosely; do not weave in ends. Length will be adjusted after couching. Ends will be used to secure Cording.

Using method of choice listed below, work two cords, each 12"/30.5 cm long for Sleeves; one cord 33"/84 cm long for neck, one cord 66"/167 cm long for lower edge between MC and Lace sections and ties.

A. Using Embellish Knit Automatic Spool Knitter, work cord, following instructions included with Knitter.

B. Using crochet hook, ch 5, join with a slip st to form a ring. Working around in a spiral, slip st in each st until cord is desired length. Fasten off.

C. Using 2 double pointed needles, work I-cord to desired lengths.

COUCH (ATTACH) CORDING

Neck Edge

1. Beginning with the cast on end of cording at right center Front, lay cording along neckline just inside sc edging.

2. Using yarn needle and C, work Cross stitch over cording, stretching cording slightly.

3. Slowly unravel cording at bind-off end to meet garment exactly, bind off.

4. Use ends of cording to secure cord to Jacket edge.

Lower Edge of MC Section

1. Beginning at right center Front, leaving approximately 12" to 14"/30.5 to 36 cm for tie, couch cording to lower edge between MC and lace sections as for neckline.

2. Leave 12" to 14"/30.5 to 36 cm for tie at left Front.

3. Unravel as for neckline. Secure loose ends inside ties and tie knot at end.

Sleeves

Attach cording to each Sleeve between MC and CC sections.

EMBROIDERY

1. Trace embroidery pattern onto tracing paper, reversing patterns for left side and left sleeve. Pin paper to Jacket and Sleeves.

2. Using embroidery needle and any color embroidery floss, work Running stitch along all pattern lines to mark. Carefully tear away tracing paper.

Helpful: Use different color of floss for leaves. Embroider patterns as shown using Stem st and C for all line work and Satin st and B for leaves.

ASSEMBLY

Sew in Sleeves; sew sleeve seams.
Using yarn needle, weave in all ends.

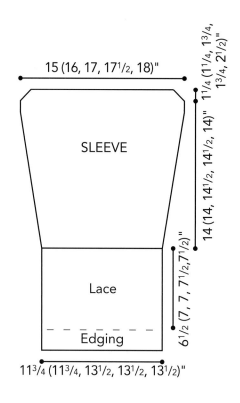

15 (16, 17, 17½, 18)"

1¼ (11¼, 1¾, 1¾, 2½)"

SLEEVE

14 (14, 14½, 14½, 14)"

Lace

6½ (7, 7, 7½, 7½)"

Edging

11¾ (11¾, 13½, 13½, 13½)"

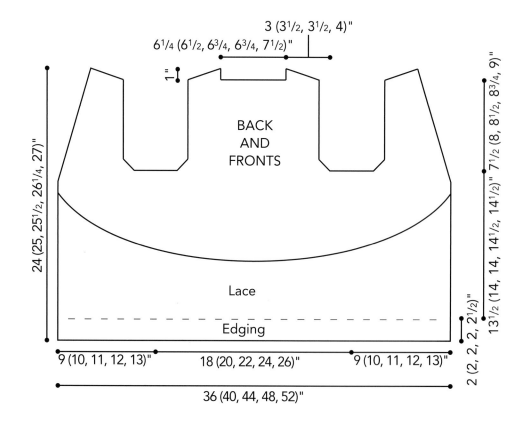

3 (3½, 3½, 4)"

6¼ (6½, 6¾, 6¾, 7½)"

1"

BACK
AND
FRONTS

7½ (8, 8½, 8¾, 9)"

24 (25, 25½, 26¼, 27)"

13½ (14, 14, 14½, 14½)"

Lace

Edging

2 (2, 2, 2½)"

9 (10, 11, 12, 13)"   18 (20, 22, 24, 26)"   9 (10, 11, 12, 13)"

36 (40, 44, 48, 52)"

Back

Sleeve

Center Back

Right Front

Orient Express

Think Indonesia and India...
sparkly, vibrant colors...
accents and embroidery...
curry, coriander, and cumin...

Kimono Shrug

DESIGNED BY TAMMY HILDEBRAND WITH CARI CLEMENT

EASY

In this easy project the embellishing is done along the fronts where the colors meet. By using different color trims and beads, you can create shrugs to go with as many outfits as you like.

SIZES

Small (Medium, Large, Extra-Large)

FINISHED MEASUREMENTS

Bust 36 (40, 44, 48)"/91.5 (101.5, 112, 122) cm

Length 18 ½"/46.5 cm, all sizes

NOTE: Shrug is loose fitting and designed to be worn as shown in photo. Bust measurements are suggested sizes for a standard fitting garment; choose accordingly. Due to shaping, garment is wider than measurements indicate on schematic.

YARN

Caron International's Simply Soft
(100% acrylic; 6 oz/170 g, 315 yds/288 m skein):

- #9730 Autumn Red (MC), 3 (3, 4, 4) skeins
- #9711 Dk. Country Blue (CC), 2 (2, 2, 2) skeins

CROCHET HOOKS

One each size US G-6 and J-10 (4 and 6 mm), or size to obtain gauge

ADDITIONAL MATERIALS

Yarn needle

1 ¼ yards/118 cm flat braid trim, ¾"/1.9 cm wide, in color desired (shown in red, with gold metallic threads)

28 textured brass beads, 4 mm x 6 mm

14 bugle beads, 11 mm long, dark red

14 glass beads, in various sizes, no smaller than 6 mm, no larger than 11 mm, dark red

Tapestry or beading needle (thin enough to fit through beads)

Beading or quilting thread to match braid

Sewing needle and thread to match garment

Straight pins or small safety pins

GAUGE

In Stitch Pattern, 12 sc and 12 rows = 4"/10 cm, using larger hook and MC; in single crochet, 13 sc and 16 rows = 4"/10 cm, using smaller hook and CC

CROCHET STITCHES USED

ch: chain

sc: single crochet

slip st: slip stitch

Stitch Pattern (Multiple of 2 sc + 1)

- ROW 1 (RS): Sc in second ch from hook and each ch across, turn.
- ROW 2: Ch 1, sc in first st, * ch 1, skip next st, sc in next st; repeat from * across, turn.
- ROW 3: Ch 1, sc in first st and in each ch-1 space and sc across, turn.
- Repeat Rows 2 and 3 for Stitch pattern.

NOTES

1. Shrug is worked from lower edge of Front, across shoulders to lower edge of Back.
2. Side Front/Sleeve is worked to shoulder; CC panels are then worked on each Front.
3. Back/Sleeves are joined at shoulders to Side Front/Sleeve and CC Panels, then worked down.
4. Cuffs are worked down from lower edge of Sleeves.

LEFT SIDE FRONT/SLEEVE

Using larger hook and MC, chain 14 (18, 22, 26).

Row 1 (RS): Work Row 1 of Stitch pattern—13 (17, 21, 25) sc.

Row 2: Work Row 2 of Stitch pattern—7 (9, 11, 13) sc; 6 (8, 10, 12) ch-1 spaces.

Row 3: Work Row 3 of Stitch pattern—13 (17, 21, 25) sc.

Rows 4–16: Work even in pattern, repeating Rows 2 and 3, end with (WS) Row 2.

SHAPE SIDE AND UNDERARM

Row 17 (RS): At side edge, ch 1, work [2 sc in first st (increase)], beginning at *, work in pattern to end, turn—14 (18, 22, 26) sc.

Row 18: Work in pattern across to last st, [ch 1, sc in last st, (increase)], turn—8 (10, 12, 14) sc; 7 (9, 11, 13) ch-1 spaces.

Rows 19–25: Work in pattern, increasing 1 st at side edge every row, turn—22 (26, 30, 34) sc.

Row 26: Work in pattern across to last st, ch 1, sc in last st; do NOT turn—12 (14, 16, 18) sc; 11 (13, 15, 17) ch-1 spaces.

SLEEVE

Chain 31, turn.

Row 27 (RS): Sc in second ch from hook and in next 29 ch; sc in next st and in each sc and ch-1 space to end—53 (57, 61, 65) sc.

Rows 28–42: Work even in pattern, end with a WS row.

SHAPE NECK

Row 43: Work in pattern across to last st, turn, [leaving last st at neck edge unworked (decrease)]—52 (56, 60, 64) sc.

Row 44: Slip st in next st (decrease), ch 1, sc in same st, work in pattern to end, turn—26 (28, 30, 32) sc; 25 (27, 29, 31) ch-1 spaces remain.

Rows 45–56: Work in pattern, decreasing 1 st at neck edge every row—20 (22, 24, 26) sc; 19 (21, 23, 25) ch-1 spaces remain at shoulder edge. Fasten off.

FRONT PANEL

With RS facing, using smaller hook and CC, join yarn with a sc in first row end of neck (at shoulder edge).

Row 1: Sc in each row end along Front edge to lower edge, turn—56 sc.

Row 2: Ch 1, sc in each st across, turn.

Rows 3–18: Work even in sc, repeating Row 2. Fasten off.

RIGHT SIDE FRONT/SLEEVE

Using larger hook and MC, chain 14 (18, 22, 26). Work as for left Front for 16 rows, end with (WS) Row 2.

SHAPE SIDE AND UNDERARM

Row 17 (RS): Work in pattern across to last st, work [2 sc in last st (increase)], turn—14 (18, 22, 26) sc.

Row 18: Ch 1, sc in first st, [ch 1, sc in next st (increase)], work in pattern to end—8 (10, 12, 14) sc; 7 (9, 11, 13) ch-1 spaces.

Rows 19–26: Work in pattern, increasing 1 st at side edge every row—12 (14, 16, 18) sc; 11 (13, 15, 17) ch-1 spaces. At front edge, drop yarn, do NOT fasten off.

SLEEVE

With RS facing, join another strand of MC with a slip st in first st of Row 26 (side edge), chain 30. Fasten off; return to front edge, pick up dropped strand of yarn.

Row 27 (RS): Work in pattern across to chain, sc in each ch to end, turn—53 (57, 61, 65) sc.

Rows 28–42: Work even in pattern, end with a WS row.

SHAPE NECK

Row 43: Slip st in next ch-1 space (decrease), ch 1, sc in same space, work in pattern to end, turn—52 (56, 60, 64) sc.

Row 44: Work in pattern across to last st, turn, leaving last st unworked (decrease)—26 (28, 30, 32) sc; 25 (27, 29, 31) ch-1 spaces.

Rows 45–56: Work in pattern, decreasing 1 st every row—20 (22, 24, 26) sc; 19 (21, 23, 25) ch-1 spaces at shoulder edge. Fasten off.

FRONT PANEL

With RS facing, using smaller hook and CC, join yarn with a sc in first row end at lower edge. Work as for left Front.

BACK

Joining Row—With RS facing, using larger hook and MC, join yarn with a slip st in first sc of left Sleeve; ch 1, work in pattern (sc in each sc and ch-1 space) across to left Front Panel; working in row ends, sc in each row end across; chain 17 for Back neck; working in row ends, sc in each row end across right Front Panel; work in pattern to end, turn—57 (61, 65, 69) sc each side of chain.

Row 2: Work in pattern across to chain; sc in each ch across Back neck; work in pattern to end, turn—29 (31, 33, 35) sc; 28 (30, 32, 34) ch-1 spaces each side, 17 sc at center Back.

Row 3: Work in pattern (sc in each sc and ch-1 space) across, turn—131 (139, 147, 155) sc.

Row 4: Work in pattern across all sts—66 (70, 74, 78) sc; 65 (69, 73, 77) ch-1 spaces.

Rows 5–29: Work even in pattern. Fasten off.

SLEEVES

Row 30 (WS): Skip first 30 sts (Sleeve); join MC with a sc in next st; work in pattern across to last 30 sts, turn, leaving last 30 sts unworked for Sleeve—36 (40, 44, 48) sc, 35 (39, 43, 47) ch-1 spaces remain.

SHAPE SIDE AND UNDERARM

Row 31: Slip st in next ch-1 space, slip st in next st (2 sts decreased); ch 1, sc in same st, work in pattern across to last 2 sts, turn, leaving remaining sts unworked (2 sts decreased)—67 (75, 83, 91) sc remain.

Row 32: Slip st in next 2 sts (2 sts decreased), ch 1, sc in same st, work in pattern across to last 2 sts, turn, leaving remaining sts unworked

(2 sts decreased—32 (36, 40, 44) sc, 31 (35, 39, 43) ch-1 spaces remain.

Rows 33–38: Continuing in pattern, decrease 2 sts each side every row 6 times, working as for Rows 31 and 32—20 (24, 28, 32) sc, 19 (23, 27, 31) ch-1 spaces remain.

Rows 39: Work even in pattern—39 (47, 55, 63) sc.

Rows 40–56: Work even in pattern. Fasten off.

FINISHING

Using yarn needle, weave in all ends.

ASSEMBLY

With WS facing each other, sew side and Sleeve seams, matching shaping.

CUFFS

Note: Work in joined rows, turning at the end of each row.

Row 1: Using smaller hook and CC, join yarn with a sc in row end at seam; sc in each row around, join with a slip st in beginning sc, turn.

Row 2: Ch 1, sc in each sc around, join with a slip st in beginning sc, turn.

Rows 3–22: Work even in sc, repeating Row 2. Fasten off.

LOWER EDGE

With WS facing, using smaller hook and CC, working in row ends of lower edge of Front Panel, join yarn with a sc in corner row of right Front Panel; sc in each row end across to Side-Front; change to MC, working in remaining loops of foundation ch, sc in each st across Front; sc in each st across Back; working as for Right Side-Front, work across Left Side-Front; change to CC, work across row ends of Left Front Panel to end. Fasten off.

EMBELLISHING

1. Separate the beads into 3 groups: bugle beads, red glass beads, and brass beads.

2. Measure distance of contrast band from shoulder to lower edge and cut trim accordingly, adding ½"/1.3 cm for turn-under.

3. Fold in ¼"/.6 cm hem at lower edge of trim and stitch.

4. Mark the trim with pins for bead placement.

5. Thread sewing needle with matching thread and bring to RS. Sew on beads as follows: brass bead, bugle bead, glass bead. Repeat in that order for the length of the trim.

6. Pin trim to Kimono over the seam and stitch in place with sewing thread.

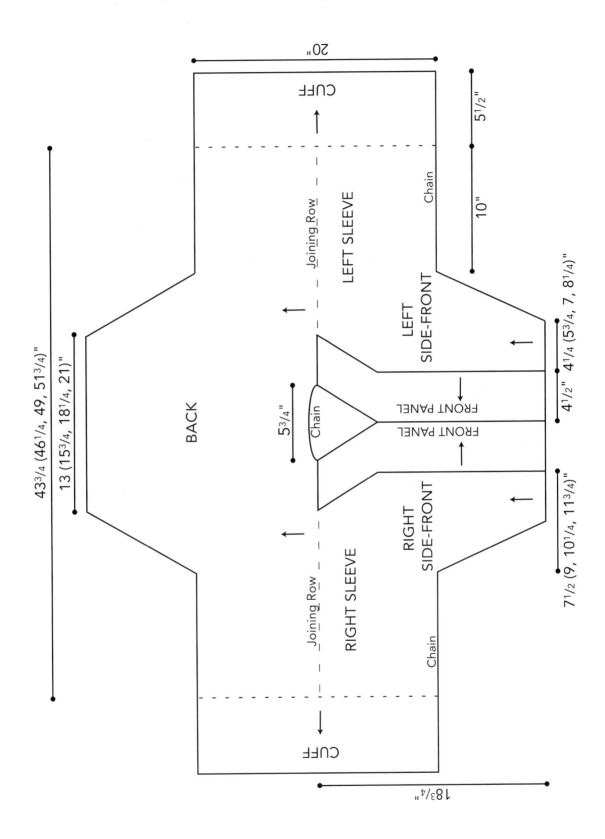

20"

CUFF

5½"

10"

Joining Row

LEFT SLEEVE

Chain

LEFT SIDE-FRONT

4¼ (5¾, 7, 8¼)"

4½"

FRONT PANEL

FRONT PANEL

5¾"

Chain

BACK

43¾ (46¼, 49, 51¾)"

13 (15¾, 18¼, 21)"

RIGHT SIDE-FRONT

7½ (9, 10¼, 11¾)"

Joining Row

RIGHT SLEEVE

Chain

CUFF

18¾"

Hobo Boho Bag

DESIGNED BY NOREEN CRONE-FINDLAY

INTERMEDIATE

Inspired by paisley motifs from India, this Hobo Bag is a great splash of color! The Tunisian crochet (Afghan stitch) creates a bag that is fun to make and a true palette for embellishments.

ONE SIZE

FINISHED MEASUREMENTS

Width 12 ½"/32 cm

Length (at center of Bag) 7"/18 cm

Strap Length 22"/56 cm

YARN

Caron International's Simply Soft
(100% acrylic; 6 oz/170 g, 315 yds/288 m skein):

- #9723 Raspberry (A), 1 skein
- #9727 Black (B), 1 skein

Caron International's Simply Soft Brites
(100% acrylic; 6 oz/170 g, 315 yds/288 m skein):

- #9605 Mango (C), 1 skein

CROCHET HOOK

One Tunisian hook size US N-15 (10 mm), or size to obtain gauge

ADDITIONAL MATERIALS

Crochet hook size US H-8 (5 mm), for embellishment

2 packages (1 yard/.92 cm each) beaded trim (2"/5 cm wide shown on model)

3 skeins gold metallic embroidery floss

30 gram tube mixed E beads

30 gram tube rocaille E beads, hot pink

Beading needle (thin enough to fit through beads)

Pins

Row counter (optional)

Ruler (for reading chart) (optional)

GAUGE

In Tunisian crochet, 10 sts and 8 rows = 4"/10 cm, using 2 strands of yarn held together

CROCHET STITCHES USED

ch: chain

hdc: half double crochet

sc: single crochet

slip st: slip stitch

NOTES

1. Use a double strand of each color throughout.
2. Each square on the Chart represents one stitch.
3. When changing colors, always bring the new color under the working color to avoid holes from forming.

HELPFUL

READING CHART: When working from Chart, place a ruler on the Chart, covering the rows above the row that is being worked.

SPECIAL TECHNIQUES

Tunisian Crochet (Afghan stitch)
Each row of Tunisian crochet is worked in two steps after the Foundation Row.

Foundation Row (counts as Step 1)
Chain the number of sts indicated in the instructions; skip first ch, * insert hook in next ch, yarn over and draw up a loop (2 loops on hook); repeat from * across, drawing up a loop in each ch. Complete Foundation Row by working Step 2. Repeat Steps 1 and 2 for remainder of piece.

STEP 1. With RS facing, working from right to left, pick up stitches for the row: Beginning in the second vertical bar of the previous row, * insert hook into the vertical bar of the previous row, yarn over and draw loop through the vertical bar (2 loops on hook); repeat from * across, drawing up a loop in each vertical bar.

STEP 2. Working from left to right, work off the stitches: Yarn over and draw through first loop on hook, * yarn over and draw through 2 loops on hook; repeat from * across.

INCREASE IN TUNISIAN CROCHET: At the beginning of Step 1, insert hook into first vertical bar; at end of Step 1, pick up 2 sts in last vertical bar.

DECREASE IN TUNISIAN CROCHET: Insert hook into 2 vertical bars, yarn over and draw loop through both vertical bars.

BAG AND STRAPS (MAKE 2)

Using Tunisian hook and 2 strands of C, working in Tunisian Crochet throughout, chain 8; join 2 strands A, chain 9. Begin working from Chart; work Rows 1—52, working each strap separately. Fasten off.

EMBELLISHING

BEAD FLOWERS (MAKE 16)

1. Cut an 18"/46 cm length of A and split it into 4 single strands (see page 15).

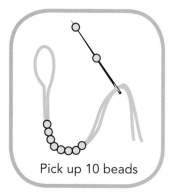

Pick up 10 beads

2. Fold one strand in half, thread ends through beading needle, and pick up 10 beads.

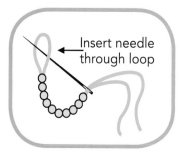

Insert needle through loop

3. Take the needle through the loop, pull up to form a ring of beads.

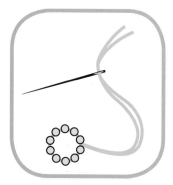

4. Pull one of the strands of yarn out of the needle; thread 7 beads onto the remaining strand and push them snugly against the bead ring.

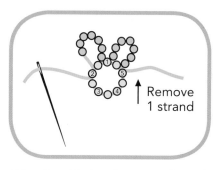

Remove 1 strand

5. Skip 1 bead in bead ring, and stitch through next bead in ring (see Diagram); repeat 4 more times to create 5 petals.

6. Stitch one flower to the center of the contrasting color motifs on both sides; scatter and stitch the other flowers randomly.

SLIP STITCH OUTLINES (CENTER OF BAG, MOTIF OUTLINES, BOTTOM EDGE OF STRAPS)

Work along lines of color changes.

1. With 2 strands of metallic embroidery floss, make a slip knot.

2. Hold slip knot and embroidery floss to WS of piece; insert hook through bag, pull up the slip knot.

3. Insert hook into Bag again, moving along the line that you want to outline, pull up a loop of yarn, pulling it through to the RS and through the loop on the hook; repeat until outline is complete. Fasten off.

FINISHING

ASSEMBLY

Lay one piece on the other, WS together.

OUTER EDGE

1. Using smaller hook and 1 strand of B, beginning at tip of one strap, work 2 sc in the row ends of the strap inner edge; working through both layers to join, continue to Chart Row 18.

2. Work 1 hdc in each st, through one layer only, to form opening of Bag.

3. At bottom of other strap (Row 18), work through both layers from Chart Row 18 to Row 52.

4. At tip of second strap, turn, ch 1, work slip st in each sc down to opening of Bag (Row 18).

5. Work 1 hdc in each st across through one layer only to form opening of bag, then slip st up to tip of first strap. Do NOT cut yarn.

EDGING

Beginning at the tip of strap, ch 2, sc evenly around outside edge of Bag, working through both layers to join front of bag to back.

ATTACHING BEADED FRINGE TRIM

1. Lay one strand of beaded trim on top of the other; join B to the outside edge of Chart Row 18.

2. Fold over 4"/10 cm of trim and pin in place at bottom edge of Strap; using B, sc over the trim to secure it, working into the sc at lower edge of Bag.

   Note: The hook will come up between the bead fringes to allow beads to hang freely.

3. Work 2 sc in corner sc to ease curves.

4. After the first side and lower edge have been worked, pin the remaining trim, folding trim end over at Chart Row 18.

5. Work over the doubled trim, finishing at the fold.

6. Cut yarn, leaving an 8"/20.5 cm tail to weave in; take tail to WS and weave in securely.

7. Join B with a slip st to opening edge of Bag; work a slip st in each hdc to stabilize opening. Cut yarn, weave in ends.

8. Tie strap tips into a knot.

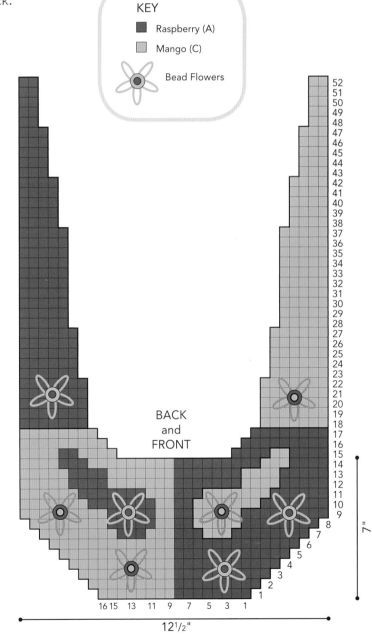

KEY

- Raspberry (A)
- Mango (C)
- Bead Flowers

BACK and FRONT

26"

12½"

7"

Wrap Jacket

DESIGNED BY MARGARET WILLSON

EASY

This Asian-inspired design is chic and quite easy to crochet, but it's the detailed embellishing that really makes this a work of art.

SIZES

Small (Medium, Large, Extra-Large)

FINISHED MEASUREMENTS

Bust 37 (41, 45, 49)"/94 (104, 114, 124.5) cm

Length 22 ½ (23, 24, 24 ½)"/ 57 (58.5, 61, 62) cm

YARN

Caron International's Simply Soft
(100% acrylic; 6 oz/170 g; 315 yds/288 m skein):

- #9748 Rubine Red (MC) 5 (6, 7, 7) skeins
- #9727 Black (A), 1 skein
- #9742 Grey Heather (B), 1 skein

CROCHET HOOKS

One each size US H-8 (5 mm), US 1-9 (5.5 mm), US J-10 (6 mm), or size to obtain gauge

ADDITIONAL MATERIALS

Yarn needle

Beading needle (thin enough to fit through beads)

Beading thread or black quilting thread

Two ⅞"/2.2 cm plastic rings

Straight pins

Safety pin

73 grams E-beads, opaque black — Bead-A

30 grams rocailles, red — Bead-B

24 grams glass spacer beads, ruby — Bead-C

30 grams E-beads, black opal — Bead-D

40 spacers, leaves, silver — Bead-E

12 metal oval barrel beads, silver — Bead-F

7 grams 11/0 round silver-lined beads, lt. gray — Bead-G

GAUGE

In Stitch pattern, using largest hook (J-10), 17 sts and 17 rows 4"/10 cm

CROCHET STITCHES USED

ch: chain

sc: single crochet

sc2tog: single crochet 2 together—insert hook in next st, yarn over and pull up a loop (2 loops on hook), insert hook in next st, yarn over and pull up loop, yarn over and draw through all 3 loops on hook.

slip st: slip stitch

Stitch Pattern (multiple of 2 sts + 1)

- ROW 1 (WS): Ch 1, sc in first sc, * sc in next ch-1 space, ch 1, skip next sc; repeat from * across until last ch-1 space, sc in next ch-1 space, sc in last sc, turn.
- ROW 2 (RS): Ch 1, sc in first sc, * ch 1, skip next sc, sc in next ch-1 space; repeat from * across to last 2 sc, ch 1, skip next sc, sc in last sc, turn.
- Repeat Rows 1 and 2 for St patt.
- NOTE: Ch-1 space counts as 1 st for counting stitches or measuring gauge.

BACK

(RS) Using medium hook (I-9) and MC, chain 82 (90, 100, 108).

Row 1: Sc in second ch from hook, * ch 1, skip next ch, sc in next ch; repeat from * across, turn—81 (89, 99, 107) sts.

(WS) Change to largest hook (J-10) and St patt; work even until piece measures 21 ¹/₂ (22, 23, 23 ¹/₂)"/54.5 (56, 58.5, 60) cm from beginning. Fasten off.

LEFT FRONT

(RS) Using medium hook and MC, ch 76 (84, 92, 102).

Row 1: Work as for Back—75 (83, 91, 101) sts. Continuing as for Back, work even until piece measures 8 ¹/₂ (8, 8, 7)"/21.5 (20.5, 20.5, 18) cm from beginning, end with a WS row.

SHAPE NECK

(RS) Beginning this row, at neck edge (end of RS rows, beginning of WS rows) dec 1 st (sc2 tog) every row 50 (54, 58, 64) times—25 (29, 33, 37) sts remain for shoulder. Work even until piece measures same as Back to shoulders. Fasten off.

RIGHT FRONT

Work as for Left Front, reversing all shaping by working neck shaping at beginning of RS rows, end of WS rows.

SLEEVE (MAKE 2)

Using medium hook and MC, ch 48 (50, 52, 54).

Row 1: Work as for Back—47 (49, 51, 53) sts. (WS) Change to largest hook and St patt; work even for 1 row.

SHAPE SLEEVE

Inc 1 st each side (work 2 sc in first st and last st of row) every 2 rows 0 (8, 14, 20) times, then every 4 rows 16 (12, 9, 6) times—79 (89, 97, 105) sts. Work even until piece measures 15 ½"/39.5 cm from beginning. Fasten off.

FINISHING

Note: It will be easier to work Part I of the embellishing before assembling garment.

EMBELLISHING—PART I

EMBROIDERY

Following Sleeve Chart and Illustrations, work Beaded Lazy Daisy stitch and Upright Cross stitch over center 27 sts of sleeve.

1. Beaded Lazy Daisy: Thread beading needle with beading thread, make Back stitch on WS to secure, * needle up at 1 (center-point), thread [Bead-A, Bead-B] six times, Bead-A, 2 Bead-B, Bead-A, [Bead-B, Bead-A] 6 times, needle down at 1 and up at 2 inside the thread, then between the 2 B-beads and down at 3; needle up at 2, thread one Bead-C, 7 Bead-G, then go back through same C-bead, needle down at 3 once more.

2. Couch (see photo) one side of petal to return to center-point 1. Repeat from * 3 more times to complete 4 petals, couch remaining strands, make Back stitch on WS to secure and cut thread.

UPRIGHT CROSS STITCH:

Using yarn needle and single strand of A, begin at bottom of Chart.

1. Secure with Back stitch on WS, * needle up at 1, down at 2, up at 3, down at 4, repeat from * for each Cross stitch, working clockwise around diamond shape.

2. Make Back stitch and secure end on WS.

ASSEMBLY

Sew shoulder seams. Measure down 9 (10, 11, 12)"/23 (25.5, 27.5, 30) cm from shoulder on Back and Fronts; place a marker for underarm. Sew Sleeves between markers; sew Sleeve and side seams.

EDGING

Round 1: With RS facing, using medium hook and A, join yarn at right-hand side seam at lower edge; ch 1, sc in same st, work [skip next st, 2 sc in next space] across to Front corner; work 3 sc in corner st; work [skip next row, 2 sc in next row] along right Front edge to beginning of neck shaping; work 2 sc in corner; work [skip next row, 2 sc in next row] along right Front neck shaping, across Back neck, and down left Front neck shaping to beginning of shaping; work 2 sc in corner; work [skip next row, 2 sc in next row] along left Front edge to lower corner; work 3 sc in corner; work [skip next st, 2 sc in next space] across to beginning of round, join with a slip st to first st; do NOT turn.

Rounds 2–5: Ch 1, sc in each sc to corner, work 3 sc in corner st, work [sc in each st to beginning of neck shaping, 2 sc in corner] twice, sc in each st to lower corner, work 3 sc in corner st, sc in each remaining st, join with a slip st to first st. Fasten off.

SLEEVE EDGING

Round 1: With RS facing, using medium hook and A, join yarn with a slip st at Sleeve seam; ch 1, sc in same st, work [skip next st, 2 sc in next space] around, join with a slip st in first st; do NOT turn.

Rounds 2–5: Ch 1, sc in each st around, join with a slip st in first st. Fasten off.

EMBELLISHING—PART II

TWISTED CORD (BODY)

1. Cut two 10-yard/9.15 m lengths of B.

2. Fold in half.

3. Knot free ends together, leaving 2"/5 cm free after knot.

4. Pin knotted end to fixed surface with safety pin.

5. Holding folded end, stand far enough away that the cord is taut, and with pencil inserted in loop formed at fold, twist until the length is evenly twisted.

6. Bring folded end and tied ends together, knot ends together.

7. Allow the strands to twirl around each other.

8. Remove safety pin.

COUCH TWISTED CORD TO BODY

1. Using crochet hook, draw one end of Cord through to WS of center Back neck, below Round 1 of edging.

2. Thread beading needle with beading thread.

3. Attach with Back stitch at WS of Back neck.

4. Needle up below twist in Cord.

5. String 1 Bead-A, 2 Bead-B, 1 Bead-D, 2 Bead-B, 1 Bead-A.

6. Needle down above twist, encasing cord.

7. Make Back stitch on WS.

8. Repeat Steps 4—7 for each twist in Cord, around entire outer edge. Fasten off.

9. Using crochet hook, draw opposite end of Cord through to WS of Back neck, beside beginning end of Cord.

10. Tie knot in Cord. Cut any excess Cord, leaving 2"/5 cm after knot.

11. With yarn needle, weave each separate strand of Cord into edging on WS of Back neck.

TWISTED CORD (SLEEVES)

1. For each Sleeve, cut two 1-yard/.9 cm lengths of B.

2. Repeat Steps 2—8 of Twisted Cord (Body).

COUCH TWISTED CORD TO SLEEVES

1. Beginning at Sleeve seam, using crochet hook, draw one end of Cord to WS at Sleeve seam.

2. Couch cord to both Sleeves as for Body.

CORDED TIES WITH RING TASSELS

Right Front Tie and Tassel

Using smallest hook (H-8) and A, leave 6"/15 cm yarn tail before making slip knot.

1. Chain 35.

2. Leaving 6"/15 cm yarn tail after chain, cut A. Fasten off.

ATTACH CORDED TIE TO RING

1. Fold chain in half.

2. Insert folded end through plastic ring, forming a loop.

3. Draw both cut ends through loop.

4. Holding the ring in one hand and cut ends in the other, pull to form a half-hitch knot.

MAKE TASSEL ON RING

Note: Bead-C includes a variety of ruby shades; refer to photo, or use your choice from mixture when directed to use Bead-C.

1. Using small hook and A, insert hook through right edge of half-hitch knot on ring and draw up loop.

2. Work 18 sc over ring, join with a slip st at left side of knot.

3. Cut A, fasten off ends securely.
4. Thread beading needle with beading thread and make Back stitch on WS of knot.
5. Thread 3 beads, 1 Bead-C, 1 Bead-A, 1 Bead-C.

6. Working counterclockwise, bring needle from WS around outer edge and down through next sc.

7. Work Back stitch on WS of same sc.
8. Repeat Steps 5—7 five more times.

9. Beaded Fringe: Back stitch on WS, needle up in next sc, thread Bead-C, Bead-F, Bead-C, Bead-A, Bead-C, Bead-A, 2 Bead-C, Bead-D, Bead-C, Bead-E; after Bead-E, thread needle up through beads to beginning, needle down in same sc.
10. Repeat Step 9 five more times.
11. Repeat Steps 5—7 six times, returning to half-hitch knot. Fasten off.

Tip: Use a small dot of fabric glue where beading thread begins and ends; knots made using nylon or silk thread have a tendency to loosen over time.

Using yarn needle, sew ends of Corded Tie to corner at beginning of neck shaping on right Front, weaving 6"/15 cm ends through edging to secure.

LEFT FRONT TIE AND TASSEL

1. Using small hook and A, leave 6"/15 cm yarn tail before making slip knot.
2. Ch 195 (215, 235, 250).
3. Leaving 6"/15 cm yarn tail after chain, cut A.

Complete as for right Front Tassel. Using yarn needle, run end of Tassel Cord through right side seam and sew securely to corner of Left Front. Weave in ends.

TO WEAR

Wrap long Hanging Cord across Back and around to Front; meeting short Hanging Cord to cinch Jacket.

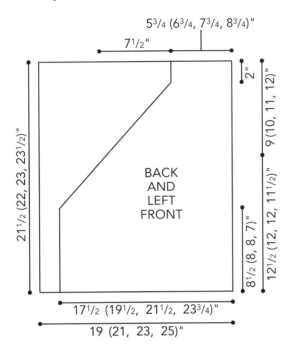

5³⁄₄ (6³⁄₄, 7³⁄₄, 8³⁄₄)"

7¹⁄₂"

2"

9 (10, 11, 12)"

BACK AND LEFT FRONT

12¹⁄₂ (12, 12, 11¹⁄₂)"

8¹⁄₂ (8, 8, 7)"

21¹⁄₂ (22, 23, 23¹⁄₂)"

17¹⁄₂ (19¹⁄₂, 21¹⁄₂, 23³⁄₄)"

19 (21, 23, 25)"

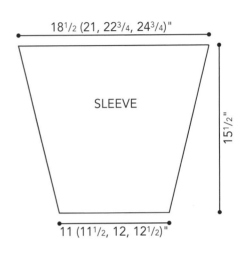

18¹⁄₂ (21, 22³⁄₄, 24³⁄₄)"

SLEEVE

15¹⁄₂"

11 (11¹⁄₂, 12, 12¹⁄₂)"

KEY

Begin Embroidery on Row 8 of Sleeve

☐ Single crochet

⊡ Chain 1 space

+ Upright Cross stitch

✍ Beaded Lazy Daisy

SLEEVE CHART

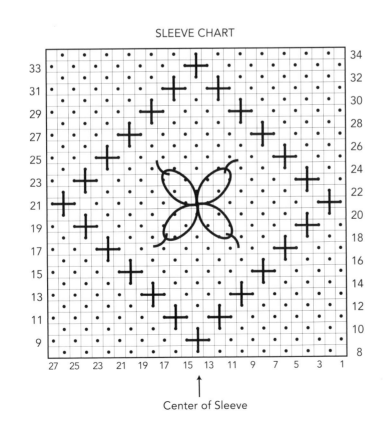

Center of Sleeve

UPRIGHT CROSS STITCH

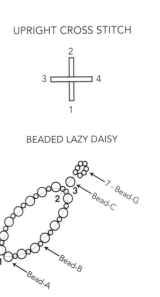

BEADED LAZY DAISY

Boho Bangles

DESIGNED BY NOREEN CRONE-FINDLAY

BEGINNER

Don't you love looking around hardware stores for something you can use in your projects? Plumbers' clear plastic tubing is ideal for these bangles, and the softness of Simply Soft makes them so comfy to wear. You can coordinate your whole wardrobe by making bangles with any color beads.

ONE SIZE

FINISHED MEASUREMENTS

Customize to fit wrist while fitting over hand.

YARN

Caron International's Simply Soft Brites (100% acrylic; 6 oz/170 g, 315 yds/288 m skein):

- #9608 Blue Mint and #9605 Mango: 1 skein each

CROCHET HOOK

One size US H-8 (5 mm)

ADDITIONAL MATERIALS

10 ½"/26.5 cm length of ¼"/.6 cm diameter clear plastic tubing for each bangle (available in aquarium section of pet store or in plumbing department of hardware store)

1 tube (30 grams) assorted glass E beads, colors to coordinate with yarn (420 beads needed)

Beading needle (thin enough to fit through beads)

Yarn needle

Fabric glue

Sharp scissors or a craft knife

Clear tape (optional)

GAUGE

Gauge is not critical to this project.

CROCHET STITCHES USED

ch: chain

sc: single crochet

NOTE

The length of tubing will determine the size of the Bangle; be sure that the length chosen will slide over hand easily. For a larger bracelet, cut a longer piece of tubing; for a smaller bracelet, cut the length shorter.

BANGLE BASE

1. Measure the circumference of a bracelet you have that fits over your wrist well plus $\frac{1}{4}$"/.6 cm.

2. Cut plastic tubing to length, allowing $\frac{1}{2}$"/1.3 cm for overlap.

3. Cut a $\frac{1}{2}$"/1.3 cm long, V-shaped notch at one end of the tubing.

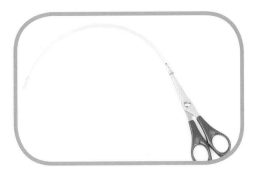

4. Push the end of scissors or a pencil into the other end to stretch the tubing slightly.

5. Push the notched end into the stretched end.

6. If desired, secure the overlap with clear tape.

EMBELLISHING

1. To reduce bulk approximately 2"/5 cm from end of yarn strand, separate 4-ply yarn into two 2-ply strands and cut off one 2-ply strand so that the yarn will fit through the eye of the beading needle; thread the remaining 2-ply strand through beading needle.

2. Fold the yarn over and glue so the threaded 2-ply ends touch the cut 4-ply ends. When the glue is thoroughly dry, thread all 420 beads onto the yarn.

3. Tie yarn to Bangle (tubing) leaving a 3"/7.5 cm tail; hold the yarn tail against the tubing and work over it so that it does not have to be woven in later.

BANGLE

1. Holding the yarn at the outer edge of tubing, [insert the hook into the center of the Bangle from front to back; yarn over and pull up a loop, pulling the hook and loop from back to front, wrapping loop around the tubing; bring the hook up to the outer edge of the hoop (where the yarn is attached)], yarn over and draw through loop on hook (first ch made).

2. Repeat from [to] (2 loops on hook), yarn over and draw through both loops on hook (sc made).

3. Slide 7 beads snugly against the hook.

4. Working over the tied-on end, repeat Steps 2 and 3 around, spiraling the stitches, until tubing is completely covered.

5. Fasten off, leaving a 6"/15 cm tail.

FINISHING

Using beading needle threaded with tail, weave tail in and out along edge of crochet to secure. Put a dot of glue on woven end; trim end. Turn the stitches so the chain is on the inside of the Bangle.

India Tunic

DESIGNED BY HEIDI STEPP

INTERMEDIATE

This comfy, unique tunic will surely garner admiration from friends and family. The beading and embellishment pattern is absolutely gorgeous and worthy of praise.

SIZES

Small (Medium, Large, 1X, 2X)

FINISHED MEASUREMENTS

Bust 36 (40, 44, 48, 52)"/91.5 (101.5, 112, 122, 132) cm

Length 31"/78.5 cm, all sizes

YARN

Caron International's Simply Soft
(100% acrylic; 6 oz/170 g, 315 yds/288 m skein):

- #9750 Chocolate (MC), 6 (7, 8, 8, 9) skeins
- #9608 Blue Mint (A), 1 skein
- #9703 Bone (B), 1 skein

CROCHET HOOKS

One each size US 1-9 (5.5 mm), US J-10 (6 mm), or size to obtain gauge

ADDITIONAL MATERIALS

Yarn needle

Sewing needle

Sewing thread to match A, B, or beads

Tapestry or sewing needle (thin enough to fit through beads)

Large-eye beading needle

Stitch markers

Straight pins

Marking pen or chalk pen in contrasting color from B

165 round beads, 6 mm, aqua semitransparent

165 seed beads, 4 mm, brown

238 seed beads, 4 mm, gold

4 wood beads, 8 mm, blue

10 wood beads, 5 mm, blue

80 shell beads, 10 mm long

GAUGE

In single crochet, 17 sts and 20 rows = 4"/10 cm, using smaller hook and B

In Stitch pattern (1 row sc, 1 row dc), 12 sts and 9.6 rows = 4"/10 cm, using larger hook and MC

NOTES

1. Beaded Yoke and Sleeve bands are worked separately, then attached to Back and Front and Sleeves.

2. Bead Embellishment will be easier to work on individual pieces, before assembly; final embroidery Embellishment is worked after Yoke and Sleeve bands have been attached.

CROCHET STITCHES USED

ch: chain

dc: double crochet

dc2tog: double crochet 2 together—
[yarn over, insert hook in next st
and pull up a loop, yarn over and
draw through 2 loops] twice, yarn
over and draw through 3 loops
on hook.

dc3tog: double crochet 3 together—
[yarn over, insert hook in next st
and pull up a loop, yarn over
and draw through 2 loops] 3
times, yarn over and draw through
4 loops on hook.

dec: decrease 1 st—work next 2 sts
together in pattern (sc2tog or
dc2tog).

dec 2: decrease 2 sts—work next
3 sts together in pattern (sc3tog
or dc2 tog)

inc: increase 1 st—work 2 sts in next
st in pattern.

sc: single crochet

sc2tog: single crochet 2 together—
insert hook in next st, yarn over
and pull up a loop (2 loops on
hook), insert hook in next st, yarn
over and pull up a loop, yarn over
and draw through all 3 loops on
hook.

sc3tog: single crochet 3 together—
[insert hook in next st, yarn over
and pull up a loop] 3 times, yarn
over and pull through all 4 loops
on hook.

slip st: slip stitch

Stitch Pattern (Body and Sleeves)

- ROW 1: Ch 1, sc in each st across.
- ROW 2: Ch 2, dc in each st across.
- Repeat Rows 1 and 2 for St patt.

BACK AND FRONT YOKE (INSERT)

Note: First 13 rows are the neckband.

Beginning at neck edge, using smaller hook and B, chain 67.

Row 1 (RS): Sc in second ch from the hook and in each ch across, turn—66 sc.

Row 2: Ch 1, work [sc in next 3 sts, inc in next st] twice, sc in next 10 sc, inc in next st, sc in next 28 sc, inc in next st, sc in next 10 sc, work [inc in next st, sc in next 3 sts] twice, turn—72 sc.

Row 3: Ch 1, sc in next 15 sc, work [inc in next st, sc in next 2 sts] twice, inc in next st, inc in next st, sc in next 24 sc, inc in next st, sc in next st, work [inc in next st, sc in next 2 sts] 3 times, turn—80 sc.

Row 4: Ch 1, inc in first st, sc in next 8 sc, inc in next st, sc in next 2 sc, inc in next st, sc in next 54 sc, inc in next st, sc in next 2 sc, inc in next st, sc in next 8 sc, inc in last st, turn—86 sts.

Row 5: Ch 1, sc in next 7 sc, inc in next st, sc in next 5 sc, inc in next st, sc in next 2 sc, inc in next st, sc in next 12 sc, inc in next st, sc in next 2 sc, inc in next st, sc in next 5 sc, inc in next st, sc in next 27 sc, turn—92 sts.

Row 6: Ch 1, sc in next 5 sc, inc in next st, sc in next 25 sc, inc in next st, sc in next 28 sc, inc in next st, sc in next 25 sc, inc in next st, sc in next 5 sc, turn—96 sc.

Row 7: Ch 1, sc in next 12 sc, inc in next st, sc in next 11 sc, inc in next st, sc in next 4 sc, inc in next st, sc in next 36 sc, inc in next st, sc in next 4 sc, inc in next st, sc in next 11 sc, inc in next st, sc in next 12 sc, turn—102 sc.

Row 8: Ch 1, sc in next st, inc in next st, sc in next 19 sc, inc in next st, sc in next 58 sc, inc in next st, sc in next 19 sc, inc in next st, sc in last sc, turn—106 sc.

Row 9: Ch 1, sc in next 18 sc, inc in next st, sc in next 15 sc, inc in next st, sc in next 36 sc, inc in next st, sc in next 15 sc, inc in next st, sc in next 18 sc, turn—110 sc.

Row 10: Ch 1, sc in next 7 sc, inc in next st, sc in next 6 sc, inc in next st, sc in next 25 sc, inc in next st, sc in next 28 sc, inc in next st, sc in next 25 sc, inc in next st, sc in next 6 sc, inc in next st, sc in next 7 sc, turn—116 sc.

Row 11: Ch 1, sc in next 38 sc, inc in next st, sc in next 38 sc, inc in next st, sc in next 38 sc, turn—118 sc.

Row 12: Ch 1, inc in first st, sc in next 15 sc, inc in next st, sc in next 14 sc, inc in next st, sc in next 7 sc, inc in next st; sc in next 12 sc, inc in next st, sc in next 12 sc, inc in next st, sc in next 12 sc, inc in next st, sc in next 7 sc, inc in next st, sc in next 14 sc, inc in next st, sc in next 15 sc, inc in last st, turn—128 sc.

Row 13: Ch 1, sc in next 28 sc, inc in next st, sc in next 70 sc, inc in next st, sc in next 28 sc, turn—130 sc.

RIGHT FRONT SHAPING

Row 14 (WS): Ch 1, work across 13 sc, turn.

Row 15: Ch 1, dec across first 2 sts, sc in next 11 sc, turn—12 sc remain.

Row 16: Ch 1, sc in next 10 sc, dec across last 2 sts, turn—11 sc remain.

Rows 17–27: Work even in sc. Fasten off.

LEFT FRONT SHAPING

With WS facing, join yarn 13 sts in from opposite edge.

Row 14: Ch 1, sc in same st and in next 12 sc, turn—13 sc.

Row 15: Ch 1, sc in next 11 sc, dec across last 2 sts, turn—12 sc remain.

Row 16: Ch 1, dec across first 2 sts, sc in next 10 sc, turn—11 sc remain.

Rows 17–27: Work even in sc.

JOINING ROW

Row 28 (WS): Continuing on Left Front, ch 1, sc in next 10 sc, inc in last st; with WS of Right Front facing, sc across (11 sts), turn—23 sc.

Rows 29–44: Work even in sc.

SHAPE TAB

Dec 1 st each side every row 10 times—3 sc.

Last Row: Ch 1, sc3tog. Fasten off.

FINISHING

Using smaller hook and A, work 1 row of sc evenly around outer and inner edges of Insert, working 3 sc in corner stitches and skipping a stitch as needed to keep work flat (see photo). Fasten off.

FRONT

Using MC and larger hook, chain 64 (70, 76, 82, 88).

Row 1 (RS): Sc in second ch from hook and each ch across, turn—63 (69, 75, 81, 87) sc.

Row 2: Ch 2, dc in first st and in each st across, turn—63 (69, 75, 81, 87) dc.

Row 3: Ch 1, sc in first st and in each st across, turn.

Work even in St patt until piece measures 5½"/14 cm from beginning.

SHAPE SIDES

Dec 1 st each side every 6 rows 4 times—55 (61, 67, 73, 79) sts.

Work even until piece measures approximately 16"/41 cm from beginning—39 rows, end with a RS row.

Begin working Side Shaping from Chart and instructions below.

Note: Shaping is mirror image on each side; Chart shows left-hand side of Front, with RS facing. Beginning Row 45 (right Front), read WS rows from right to left, RS rows from left to right.

Row 42 (WS): Inc 1 st each side—57 (63, 69, 75, 81) sts.

Work 1 row even, placing a marker on center st.

RIGHT FRONT

Divide for Neck and Insert Opening.

Row 44 (WS): Work across to 3 sts before center st, dc3tog, turn, leaving remaining sts unworked—26 (29, 32, 35, 39) sts.

Row 45: At neck edge, ch 1, dec across first 2 sts, sc in each st across, turn—1 st decreased.

Row 46: Ch 2, inc 0 (0, 0, 0, 1) st, dc across to last 3 sts, dc3tog at neck edge, turn—2 sts decreased.

Continue Neck and Side Shaping as established from Chart, and AT THE SAME TIME,

SHAPE ARMHOLES

Beginning Row 55 (53, 53, 51, 49), dec 1 (0, 1, 0, 1) st each side once, then 2 sts each side every row 3 (4, 4, 5, 5) times, working dc2tog or dc3tog as appropriate—14 (16, 18, 20, 22) sts remain when armhole shaping is complete. Work armhole edge even while completing neck shaping.

SHAPE SHOULDERS

Row 74: Slip st across 2 (3, 4, 5, 6) sts, sc to end. Fasten off.

LEFT FRONT

Row 44: With WS facing, skip center st, join yarn with a slip st in next st; ch 2, dc3tog in this and next 2 sts, dc in each st across, turn—26 (29, 32, 35, 39) sts.

Work as for right Front, reversing all shaping. Fasten off.

BACK

Work as for Front, for 42 rows, ending with a WS row. Continue working side and armhole shaping from Chart and written instructions; do NOT divide for neck shaping. Work even until Row 66 is completed, end with a WS row.

SHAPE NECK

Right Back Neck and Shoulder

Row 67 (RS): Ch 1, sc in next 11 (13, 15, 17, 19) sts, dec across next 2 sts, turn, leaving remaining sts unworked—12 (14, 16, 18, 20) sts.

Row 68: At neck edge, slip st in first two sts, ch 2, dec, work to end, turn—9 (11, 13, 15, 17) sts remain.

Row 69: Ch 1, work across to last 4 sts, dec, turn, leaving remaining 2 sts unworked—6 (8, 10, 12, 14) sts remain.

Row 70: Ch 2, dec, work to end, turn—5 (7, 9, 11, 13) sts remain.

Row 71: Ch 1, sc across to last 2 sts, dec, turn—4 (6, 8, 10, 12) sts remain.

Work even for 2 rows.

SHAPE SHOULDERS

Work as for Front. Fasten off.

LEFT NECK AND SHOULDER

With RS facing, join yarn 13 (15, 17, 19, 21) sts from left armhole edge; ch 1, dec in same and next st, sc in each st across, turn—12 (14, 16, 18, 20) sts.

Row 68: Ch 2, dc in each st across to last 4 sts, dec across next 2 sts, turn, leaving remaining sts unworked—9 (11, 13, 15, 17) sts remain.

Row 69: Slip st in first two sts, dec, sc in each st across, turn—6 (8, 10, 12, 14) sts remain sts.

Row 70: Ch 2, dc across to last 2 sts, dec, turn—5 (7, 9, 11, 13) sts remain.

Row 71: Ch 1, dec, sc across, turn—4 (6, 8, 10, 12) sts remain.

Work even for 2 rows.

SHAPE SHOULDERS

Work as for Front. Fasten off.

SLEEVE (MAKE 2)

Using MC and larger hook, chain 44.

Row 1: Sc in second ch from hook and in each ch across, turn—43 sc.

Row 2: Ch 2, dc in each st across, turn.

Row 3: Work even in pattern.

Row 4: Continuing in pattern, dec 1 st at each side this row, then every 5 (7, 7, 7, 7) rows 2 (1, 1, 1, 1) times—37 (39, 39, 39, 39) sts remain.

Work even for 4 (4, 4, 2, 2) rows. Inc 1 st at each side this row then every 5 (4, 4, 3, 3) rows 4 (6, 6, 9, 10) times—47 (53, 53, 57, 61) sts. Work even until sleeve measures 16 ½ (17 ½, 17 ½, 18, 18)"/42 (44, 44, 46, 46) cm from beginning, end with a WS row.

SHAPE CAP

Dec 1 st at each side every row 6 (6, 6, 6, 7) times—35 (41, 41, 45, 47) sts remain. Fasten off.

SLEEVE BAND (MAKE 2)

Beginning at lower edge of Sleeve band, using smaller hook and B, chain 66.

Row 1: Sc in second ch from hook and in each ch across, turn—65 sts.

Row 2: Ch 1, sc in each st across, turn.

Rows 3–7: Work even in sc.

Row 8: Dec 1 st each side, turn—63 sts remain.

Rows 9–13: Work even in sc. Fasten off.

BAND EDGING

With right sides together, sew seam; turn right side out. With RS facing, using smaller hook and A, join yarn with a slip st at seam; ch 1, work 1 row of sc around both edges of each band. Fasten off.

FINISHING

ASSEMBLY

Sew shoulder seams.

EMBELLISHING

YOKE INSERT

1. Measure 4"/10 cm from center Fronts around inside neck edge and place markers for shoulder seams.

2. Measure 15 ½"/39.5 cm around outer edges of Yoke beginning at lowest center front point and place markers at shoulder seams.

3. Fold Yoke in half and place marker at upper and lower center Back.

EMBELLISH YOKE AND SLEEVE BANDS

1. Using Yoke and Sleeve Band illustrations as a guide, with a marking pen or chalk, mark the blue curved lines and circles on all pieces.

2. Thread tapestry needle with A and work Stem stitch (see illustrations on page 128) along marked curved lines and circles.

RANDOM BEADS ALONG STEM STITCH

Using sewing thread that matches the color of the bead, sew on beads along the edges of the Stem stitch, using photo above as guide.

BEAD FLOWER

1. Thread 6 seed beads onto sewing needle threaded with sewing thread matching color B, leaving a 6"/15 cm end of thread.

2. Tie threads together to form a circle. Cut thread, leaving a 6"/15 cm end.

3. Thread sewing needle with one end of the thread and attach beads to inside of stem-stitched circle. Make a stitch across the top and bottom of the circle of seed beads. Sew a seventh seed bead to the center of the beaded circle. Secure ring of beads with 1 or 2 more stitches as needed.

INNER CIRCLE AROUND BEAD FLOWER

Thread tapestry needle with MC and work Stem stitch circle between Bead Flower and outer circle in A.

SHELL FLOWER

1. Cut two 10"/25.5 cm long lengths of sewing thread and thread through beading needle. Thread through shell bead.
2. Repeat above for each shell bead.

3. Using thread that matches the bead, sew a turquoise bead into position in center.
4. Then sew the shell beads into position using the sewing thread following illustrations and photo on page 123.

5. Thread tapestry needle with MC and work Lazy Daisy stitch around shell bead to complete Shell Flowers.

ATTACH YOKE TO FRONT

1. Match shoulder seam markers of Yoke to shoulder seams, and lower point of Yoke to center Front.
2. Pin Yoke, RS facing, onto RS of Front, overlapping Edging over Front; turn to WS.
3. Divide MC into a 2-ply strand and rethread tapestry needle. Overcast Yoke to Front, inserting needle in sts of first sc row of Yoke.

ATTACH YOKE TO BACK

Pin Insert, RS facing, onto RS of Back, matching centers and overlapping Edging over Back; turn to WS. Attach as for Front.

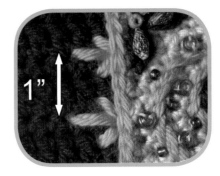

YOKE EDGING EMBROIDERY

With RS facing, using A and tapestry needle, with Short and Long sts all around outer edges of Yoke, spaced groups 1"/2.5 cm apart (see photo above and Illustrations).

Set in sleeves, matching shaping; sew Sleeve and side seams.

SLEEVE BANDS

1. Embellish bands as for Yoke, following the chart for Sleeve Bands.
2. With RS facing, pin top of Sleeve Band to lower edge of Sleeve, overlapping Band Edging over lower Sleeve edge.

3. Attach as for Front and Back Yoke.
4. With RS facing, using A and a tapestry needle, work Short and Long sts all around

upper edge of Bands, spaced 1"/2.5 cm apart (see photo on page 123 and Illustrations). Weave in all ends.

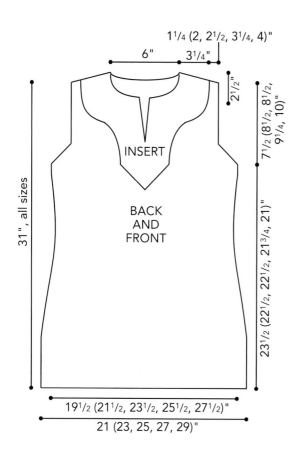

31", all sizes

1¼ (2, 2½, 3¼, 4)"

6"   3¼"

2½"

INSERT

7½ (8½, 8½, 9¼, 10)"

BACK
AND
FRONT

23½ (22½, 22½, 21¾, 21)"

19½ (21½, 23½, 25½, 27½)"
21 (23, 25, 27, 29)"

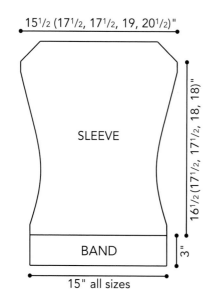

15½ (17½, 17½, 19, 20½)"

SLEEVE

16½ (17½, 17½, 18, 18)"

BAND

3"

15" all sizes

FRONT AND BACK YOKE (INSERT)

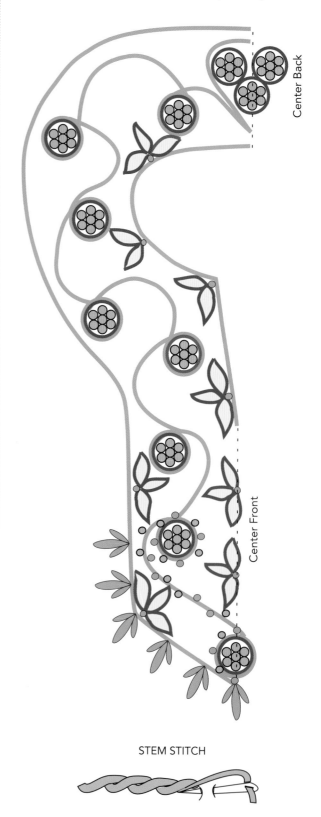

Center Back

Center Front

STEM STITCH

SLEEVE BAND

NECK, SIDE, AND ARMHOLE SHAPING CHART

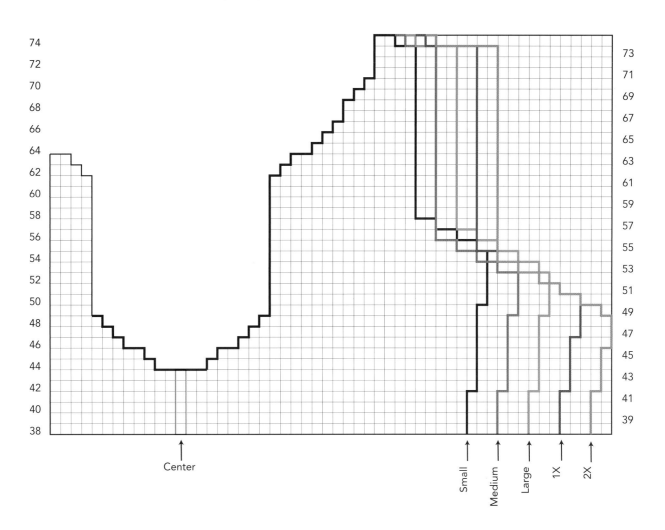

Evening Elegance

Think understated opulence …
dinner at eight…
country concerts…
evenings at the symphony…

Opera Shrug

DESIGNED BY NOREEN CRONE-FINDLAY

INTERMEDIATE

Using an easy filet crochet stitch, you can use this shrug as either a hip fashion accessory or a casual layering piece, all depending on the color of Simply Soft you choose. The band is ideal for highlighting the beaded flowers and adding that extra flair to this versatile top.

SIZES

Small (Medium, Large)

FINISHED MEASUREMENTS

Bust 36 (40, 44)"/91.5 (101.5, 112) cm

Length 18"/45.5 cm, all sizes

NOTE: Filet crochet produces a very flexible fabric—sizes are approximate.

YARN

Caron International's Simply Soft
(100% acrylic; 6 oz/170 g, 315 yds/288 m skein):

- #9727 Black, 2 (3, 3) balls

CROCHET HOOK

One size US H/8 (5 mm), or size to obtain gauge

ADDITIONAL MATERIALS

One steel crochet hook, size 10 (1 mm), for edging

Two 30-gram tubes E beads, black opal

One 30-gram tube E beads, black

One spool black thread

Beading needle

GAUGE

In filet crochet, 6 mesh sts and 6 rows = 4"/10 cm

CROCHET STITCHES USED

ch: chain

dc: double crochet

dt: double treble crochet—yarn over hook 3 times, insert hook into st indicated, yarn over and pull up a loop, [yarn over and draw through 2 loops] 4 times.

hdc: half double crochet

mesh st: mesh stitch—dc, ch 2; next dc completes one mesh.

sc: single crochet

slip st: slip stitch

tr: treble crochet—yarn over hook twice, insert hook into st indicated, yarn over and pull up a loop, [yarn over and draw through 2 loops] 3 times.

SPECIAL TECHNIQUES

Decrease in Filet Crochet

- At the beginning of a row, slip st in the back bar of the [ch-2 and dc] of the first space
- At the end of a row, do not work the last space.

Increase in Filet Crochet

- At the beginning of a row, ch 7, then dc in the top of the last dc.
- At the end of a row, ch 2, then work a dtr into the base of the last dc.

NOTES

1. The Shrug is worked in one piece in filet crochet, following Shrug Chart; Cuffs are worked following Cuff Chart.
2. The edging is worked after side edges are joined.

WORKING FILET CROCHET FROM CHARTS

1. Each square represents one mesh space (mesh stitch) in filet crochet.
2. When working from Charts, place a ruler on the Chart covering the rows above the row that you are working on. When you finish Row 1, slide the ruler up to reveal Row 2, and so on.
3. Odd-numbered rows are read from the right to left; even-numbered rows from the left to right.

BACK

Chain 7.

Foundation Row: Dc in seventh ch from hook, ch 5, dc in base of dc, * turn, ch 5, skip 2 ch, dc in next ch; repeat from * until there are 14 (20, 26) mesh sts, turn.

Begin working from Shrug Chart; work Rows 1—13, shaping as indicated and turning at the end of each row.

SLEEVES

Rows 14 and 15: Continuing from Shrug Chart, ch 25 for foundation of Sleeve; dc in eighth ch from the hook, * ch 2, skip 2 ch, dc in next ch; repeat from * five times, ch 2, dc in last dc of previous row; continue in pattern as established across.

FRONTS

Following Chart, work to beginning of neck shaping. Work across to neck edge, turn. Work each Front separately, following Chart, shaping neck, Sleeves and Front as indicated. Fasten off. Using yarn needle, weave in ends.

CUFFS (MAKE 2)

Chain 7.

Work Foundation Row as for Back until there are 8 mesh sts.

Begin working from Cuff Chart; work Rows 1—6, shaping as indicated and turning at the end of every row.

Rows 7–14: Work each side of Cuff separately.

Row 15: Work across to center; rejoin into one piece and complete Chart.

FINISHING

SIDE SEAMS

With RS facing, join yarn with a slip st at side on last row of one Front (Row 58 of Chart); ch 3, slip st in side edge mesh st of Back (Row 1 of Chart), * ch 3, slip st in next mesh st of Front, ch 3, slip st in next mesh st of Back; repeat from *, working back and forth between the edge pieces to end of Sleeves. Fasten off. Repeat for remaining seam.

FRONT BAND—SHRUG

Round 1: With RS facing, join yarn with a slip st at one side seam on lower edge; ch 2, work 3 hdc in each ch-2 space around lower edge, center Fronts and neck edge, join with a slip st to first st.

Rounds 2 and 3: Ch 2, hdc in each hdc around, join with a slip st in first st. Fasten off.

EDGING—CUFFS

Join yarn with a slip st in any ch-2 space on outer edge; ch 2, work 3 hdc into each ch-2 space around edge of cuff, join with a slip st to top of beginning ch-2. Fasten off. Weave in ends.

EMBELLISHING

BEAD EDGING—CUFFS

1. Mix one-half of the black E-beads and one-half of the black opal E-beads in a container, then randomly thread onto a strand of black sewing machine thread; using steel hook, join the thread to the outside edge of the cuff.

2. With WS facing (so beads with be on the RS when edging is completed), ch 2, * in next hdc, work [2 sc, slip bead, 2 sc] all in same st; repeat from * around, join with a slip st in first st.

3. Fasten off. Weave end securely into band.

JOIN CUFFS TO SLEEVES

After completing bead edging on Cuffs, join to Sleeves in the same manner as side seams. Join yarn with a slip st at Sleeve seam; * ch 3, slip st to mesh st on Cuff, ch 3, slip st to mesh st on Sleeve; repeat from * around.

BEAD EDGING—SHRUG

1. Thread remaining E-beads onto black sewing machine thread; using steel hook, join the thread to the outside edge of the front band.

2. With WS facing, ch 2, * in next hdc, work [2 sc, slip bead, 2 sc] all in same st; repeat from * around, join with a slip st in first st.

3. Fasten off. Weave end securely into band.

BEAD FLOWERS

1. Using remaining beads, make Bead Flowers; see instructions and Illustrations for Hobo Boho bag, page 112.

2. Make as many Bead Flowers as desired.

3. Stitch the Bead Flowers to the Front bands, and 1 on each Cuff.

Cuff chart

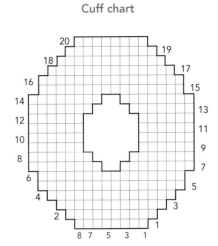

Shrug chart

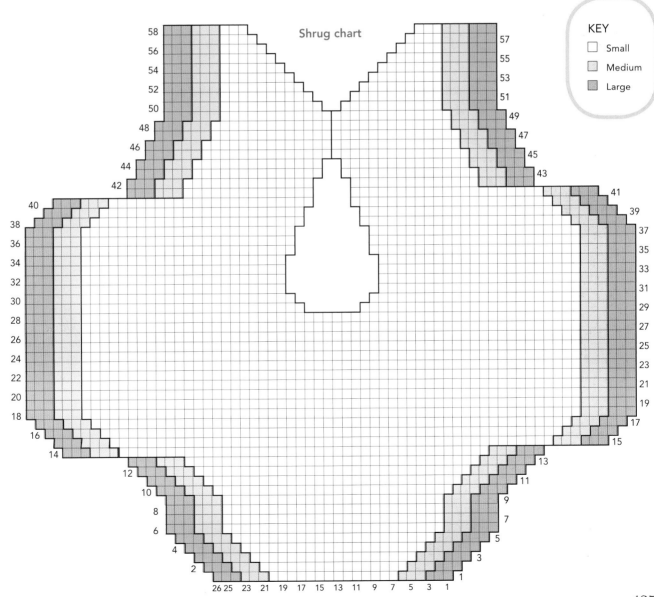

KEY

☐ Small

▨ Medium

▨ Large

Drama Necklace

DESIGNED BY NOREEN CRONE-FINDLAY

EASY

This easy-to-make necklace made from chained chains is embellished with multiple types of beads, and is sure to add a gorgeous and elegant touch to any outfit.

ONE SIZE

FINISHED MEASUREMENTS

Necklace shown measures approximately 20"/51 cm to the end of the longest strand.

YARN

Caron International's Fabulous (100% nylon; 1.76 oz/50 g, 160 yds/146 m ball):

- #0013 Country Cottage, 1 ball

CROCHET HOOK

One size US H-8 (5 mm)

ADDITIONAL MATERIALS

Two safety pins or small stitch holders

Beading or quilting thread

Sewing or beading needle (small enough to fit through beads), with a sharp point

6, 8 x 10 mm rectangular silver beads

Approx. 100 large (10 mm to 20 mm) glass beads in assorted shapes in shades of gray, black, silver, tan, and brown

Approx. 200 small (#3 seed to 6 mm) glass beads in assorted neutral colors

Steel crochet hook size US 11 (.75mm) (optional)

GAUGE

Gauge is not critical for this project.

CROCHET STITCH USED

ch: chain

NOTE

The necklace is created from 4 Cords (chained chains), which are made by working a chain with one strand of yarn, and then chaining the chain (using it as if it were a strand of yarn) to form the Cord. When the Cords are completed, they're embellished with beads of your choice, using either or both of the Beading Techniques that follow.

5. Place last ch on holder as before; remove the holder from the last chain of the Cord, and *chain the chain* to the desired length.

6. When the desired length is reached, unravel any excess chain, cut yarn, leaving a tail long enough to weave into cord and secure. Fasten off.

BEADING TECHNIQUES

1. To attach beads with small holes to the Cords, use Beading Technique One.

2. To attach beads with slightly larger holes, use Beading Technique Two, if desired.

3. To add large-hole beads, slide them onto the Cords.

BEADING TECHNIQUE ONE

1. Place the beads in a shallow bowl or jar lid.

2. Thread the beading needle; work a couple of stitches into the Cord to secure the thread.

3. Pick up a bead with the tip of the needle, slide down against the Cord.

4. Stitch through the Cord to secure the bead; work small sts into the Cord for approximately 1/2"/1.3 cm from the bead.

5. Repeat Steps 3 and 4, adding beads every 1/2"/1.3 cm along the length of the Cord.

6. Fasten off thread and weave end into Cord.

BEADING TECHNIQUE TWO (OPTIONAL)

1. Place the beads in a shallow bowl or jar lid.

2. Tie the thread to the Cord securely, leaving an end long enough to weave in.

3. Using the steel hook and attached strand of thread, work 7—9 chains; attach thread chain to Cord with a sc; remove hook from loop, enlarging the loop slightly; insert hook into the hole of a bead, slide the bead onto the hook, pick up the loop of thread with the

NECKLACE

CORDS (CHAINED CHAINS)

Make 4, each between 35" and 40"/88 and 102 cm in length.

Using larger hook and 1 strand of yarn, chain 100. Do NOT fasten off. Remove hook from last chain; place the last chain on a holder or safety pin.

1. Return to the beginning of the chain just worked (the opposite end from the holder); using larger hook, insert hook into the center of the first ch stitch.

2. Using the length of chain as if it were a strand of yarn, yarn over and pull up a loop; continue to *chain the chain* until the stitch holder is reached; do NOT fasten off.

3. Measure the Cord (chained chain); if it's not the desired length, place the last chain worked on a holder.

4. Remove the first holder (on the original chain); using larger hook and strand of yarn attached to the original chain, work additional chains.

hook and pull it through the hole in the bead; attach thread and bead to Cord with a sc.

4. Repeat Step 3, adding beads every ½"/1.3 cm along the length of the Cord.

5. Fasten off thread and weave end into Cord.

EMBELLISH NECKLACE

1. Working each Cord separately, attach beads to the Cords, using Beading Method of choice.

2. Stitch large beads to both ends of each Cord, one at a time.

3. Fold each Cord in half, gathering the center of the Cords together with a temporary tie to hold them in place while making the Tassel on the ends; ends will not all be exactly the same length.

4. Using beading thread, tie the ends together, 4" or 5" (10—12 cm) up from the ends, to form a Tassel; wrap yarn around Tassel, 1½"—2"/3.5—5 cm below where they are tied together, forming the neck of the Tassel.

5. Using needle and thread, attach beads around the wraps; fasten off securely.

6. Weave any remaining loose ends inside the Cords, stitching in place to secure.

7. Remove temporary tie around the center of the Cords.

Evening Capelet

DESIGNED BY TREVA G. MCCAIN

INTERMEDIATE

This lacy, beautiful capelet is sure to grab attention and admirers. The beaded yoke adds a feminine and delicate touch to this outstanding garment.

SIZES

Small (Medium, Large)

FINISHED MEASUREMENTS

Chest/around upper arms 41 (44, 47)"/
103 (110, 118) cm

Length 16"/40 cm

YARN

Caron International's Simply Soft
(100% acrylic; 6 oz/170 g, 315 yds/288 m skein):
- #9721 Victorian Rose, 2 skeins

CROCHET HOOK

One size US H-8 (5 mm), or size to obtain gauge

ADDITIONAL MATERIALS

Floss threader

182 (196, 210) beads with hole large enough to
   accommodate yarn

Yarn needle

GAUGE

In half double crochet, 18 sts and 11 rows = 4"/10 cm

CROCHET STITCHES USED

bc: bead chain (see page 12)

bhdc: bead half double crochet—work as bsc,
   working hdc instead of sc.

ch: chain

dc: double crochet

hdc: half double crochet

sc: single crochet

slip st: slip stitch

Lace Pattern (multiple of 14 sts)

- ROW 1: Dc in third ch from hook (counts as first 2 dc), dc in next ch, * skip 3 ch, ch 3, sc in the next 5 ch, skip 3 ch, ch 3, dc in next 3 ch; repeat from * across to last 3 ch, dc in last 3 ch, turn.
- ROW 2: Ch 3 (counts as dc, ch 1), * skip 3 dc, work 3 dc in ch-3 space, skip sc, ch 3, sc in next 3 sc, skip next sc, ch 3, work 3 dc in ch-3 space; repeat from * across, end skip 2 dc, ch 1, dc in turning ch, turn.
- ROW 3: Ch 2 (counts as dc), * dc in ch-1 space, skip 3 dc, ch 3, work 3 dc in ch-3 space, skip next sc, ch 3, dc in next sc, skip next sc, ch 3, work 3 dc in ch-3 space, skip 3 dc, ch 3; repeat from * across, end dc in ch-1 space (turning ch), dc in second ch of turning ch-3, turn.
- ROW 4: Ch 1, sc in next 2 dc, * sc in ch-3 space, skip 3 dc, ch 3, work 3 dc in ch-3 space, skip next dc, ch 1, work 3 dc in ch-3 space, skip 3 dc, ch 3, sc in ch-3 space, sc in dc; repeat from * across, end with sc in ch-3 space, sc in dc, sc in turning ch, turn.
- ROW 5: Ch 1, * sc in next 3 sc, sc in ch-3 space, ch 3, skip 3 dc, work 3 dc in ch-1 space, ch 3, skip 3 dc, sc in ch-3 space; repeat from * across, end sc in ch-3 space, sc in next 3 sc, skip turning ch, turn.
- ROW 6: Ch 1, * sc in next 3 sc, skip next sc, ch 3, work 3 dc in ch-3 space, skip 3 dc, ch 1, work 3 dc in ch-3 space, skip next sc, ch 3; repeat from * across, end sc in next 3 sc, skip turning ch, turn.
- ROW 7: Ch 2 (counts as dc), dc in second sc, * skip sc, ch 3, work 3 dc in ch-3 space, skip 3 dc, ch 3, dc in ch-1 space, skip 3 dc, ch 3, work 3 dc in ch-3 space, skip sc, ch 3, dc in sc; repeat from * across, end skip next sc, dc in next 2 sc, skip turning ch, turn.
- ROW 8: Ch 2, skip 2 dc, * ch 1, work 3 dc in ch-3 space, skip 3 dc, ch 3, sc in ch-3 space, sc in dc, sc in ch-3 space, skip 3 dc, ch 3, work 3 dc in ch-3 space, skip next dc; repeat from * across, end ch 1, dc in turning ch, turn.
- ROW 9: Ch 2 (counts as dc), work 2 dc in ch-1 space, * skip 3 dc, ch 3, sc in ch-3 space, sc in next 3 sc, sc in ch-3 space, skip 3 dc, ch 3, work 3 dc in ch-1 space; repeat from * across, end work 3 dc in ch-1 space, skip turning ch-2, turn.
- Repeat Rows 2–9 for pattern.

NOTE

Thread 26 (28, 30) beads at the beginning of each bead row to complete beading for that entire row.

YOKE

Thread beads for first row; chain 81 (87, 93).

Row 1 (WS): Hdc in third ch from hook (counts as first 2 hdc), * bhdc in next ch, hdc in next 2 ch; repeat from * across, turn—80 (86, 92) hdc, 26 (28, 30) beads.

Row 2: Ch 2 (counts as first hdc), hdc in next st, * work 3 hdc in next st, hdc in next 2 sts; repeat from * across, turn—132 (142, 152) hdc.

Row 3: Thread beads; ch 2 (counts as first hdc), hdc in next 2 sts, bhdc in next st, * hdc in next 4 sts, bhdc in next st; repeat from * across to last 3 sts, hdc in last 3 sts, turn.

Row 4: Ch 2 (counts as first hdc), hdc in each st across, turn.

Row 5: Repeat Row 3.

Row 6: Ch 2 (counts as first hdc), hdc in next 2 sts, work 3 hdc in next st, * hdc in next 4 sts, work 3 hdc in next st; repeat from * across to last 3 sts, hdc in last 3 sts, turn—184 (198, 212) hdc.

Row 7: Thread beads; ch 2 (counts as first hdc), hdc in next 3 sts, bhdc in next st, * hdc in next 6 sts, bhdc in next st; repeat from * across to last 4 sts, hdc in last 4 sts, turn.

Row 8: Repeat Row 4.

Rows 9–13: Repeat Rows 7 and 8 twice, then Row 7 once.

Row 14: Repeat Row 4, increasing 12 stitches, evenly spaced across—196 (210, 224) hdc.

BODY

Begin Lace pattern; work even for 21 rows as follows: Work Rows 1—9 once, Rows 2—9 once, then Rows 2—5 once.

EDGING

Round 1 (RS): Ch 1, * sc in each sc across to ch-3, ch 3, skip [ch-3 and next dc], work 5 dc in next dc, ch 3, skip [next dc and ch-3]; repeat from * across to the last 4 sc, sc in each of the next 3 sc, work 3 sc in last sc (corner); work 34 evenly spaced sc along Front edge, work 3 sc in first ch of beginning ch (corner); working in remaining loops of beginning ch, sc in each ch across to last ch, work 3 sc in last ch (corner), work 34 evenly spaced sc along Front edge, work 2 sc in same sc as beginning sc, join with a slip st to beginning sc.

Round 2: Ch 2 (counts as sc, ch 1), * sc in next st, ch 1; repeat from * around, join with a slip st to second ch of beginning ch-2. Fasten off.

FINISHING

Using yarn needle, weave in all ends.

TIE (MAKE 2)

Cut a strand of yarn 72"/183 cm long. Thread one end of yarn through upper Front corner of Capelet; pull through until ends of yarn are even. Thread 12 beads onto strands; working with both strands of yarn, ch 2, * bc, ch 2; repeat from * eleven times, ch 2. Fasten off. Repeat for opposite side.

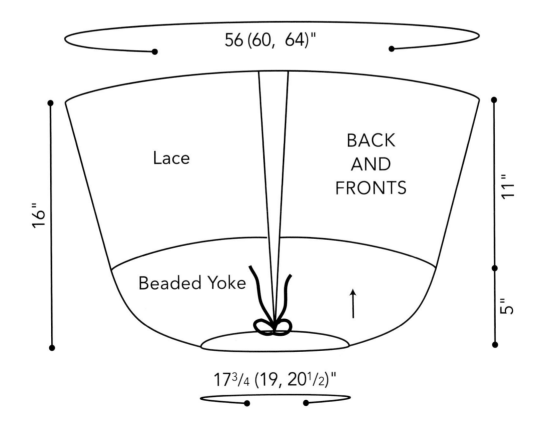

Opera Purse

DESIGNED BY CARI CLEMENT

INTERMEDIATE

Whether it's for the opera or the office, this purse is made in sections and is a great way to try your hand at bead crochet. The plastic canvas works perfectly as a purse liner by giving the purse dimension that allows you to carry your wallet, cell phone (oops, not at the opera . . .), and makeup kit without sagging.

ONE SIZE

FINISHED MEASUREMENTS

Width (lower edge) 13 ½"/34 cm;
   (upper edge) 6 ¾"/17 cm

Height 7 ½"/19 cm

Depth 2 ½"/6 cm

YARN

Caron International's Simply Soft
(100% acrylic; 6 oz/170 g, 315 yds/288 m skein):

- #9727 Black, 1 skein

CROCHET HOOKS

One each size US F-5 (3.75 mm) and US G-6 (4 mm), or size to obtain gauge

ADDITIONAL MATERIALS

Split-ring stitch marker

One pair black plastic purse handles, with slots in lower ends

Two sheets black plastic canvas, 10" x 14"/25.5 x 35.5 cm (for lining)

One vial (30 grams) glass E beads, Iris Iridescent

One 3"/7.5 cm black rayon tassel

Yarn needle

#16 tapestry needle

Scissors

Beading needle or floss threader

Straight pins

GAUGE

Gauge is not critical for this project.

In half double crochet (hdc), using larger hook, 15 sts and 8 rows = 4"/10 cm

CROCHET STITCHES USED

bc: bead chain (see page 12)

bsc: bead single crochet (see page 12)

bss: bead slip stitch (see page 13)

ch: chain

hdc: half double crochet

sc: single crochet

slip st: slip stitch

FRONT AND BACK (MAKE 2)

Using larger hook, chain 54.

Row 1: Hdc in third ch from hook and in each ch across—52 hdc.

Row 2: Ch 2, hdc in each hdc across.

Row 3: Ch 2, skip first hdc, hdc in each st across to last st, turn, leaving remaining st unworked—50 hdc.

Repeat Row 3 twelve times, dec 1 st each side every row until 26 hdc remain.

Work even, if necessary, until piece measures 7 ½"/19.5 cm from beginning. Fasten off.

BOTTOM AND SIDE GUSSETS

Using larger hook, ch 12.

Row 1: Hdc in third ch from hook and in each ch across—10 hdc.

Row 2: Ch 2, hdc in each hdc across.

Repeat Row 2 until piece measures 28 ½"/72 cm or matches measurement along sides and lower edge of Purse Front. Fasten off.

FLAP

Using beading needle or floss threader, thread yarn with 124 beads; slide beads along yarn until needed. Beginning at upper edge, using smaller hook, chain 14.

Row 1 (WS): Work bsc in second ch from hook and in each ch across, turn—13 sc.

Row 2 and all even-numbered rows: Ch 1, slip st in each sc across, turn.

Row 3: Ch 1, work 2 bsc in first st, work bsc in each st across to last st, work 2 bsc in last st—15 sc.

Row 5: Repeat Row 3—17 sc; place a marker (pm) for lower corner of Flap.

Row 7: Ch 1, skip first st, work bsc in each st across to last st, turn leaving last st unworked—15 sc.

Rows 9, 11, 13, 15, 17, 19, and 21: Repeat Row 7—1 st remains. Fasten off.

EDGING

With RS facing, using smaller hook, join yarn with a slip st to lower corner of Flap, ready to work along the shaped side edge.

Row 1 (RS): Ch 2, work 13 hdc along side edge to point; work 3 hdc in point, place a marker (pm) in center st; work 13 hdc along remaining side to opposite corner, turn.

Row 2: Ch 2, hdc in each hdc to marked st; work 3 hdc in marked st, move marker to center st; hdc to end, turn.

Repeat Row 2 until Edging measures 1 ½"/3.5 cm from the beginning, end with a RS row. Fasten off.

BEAD EDGING

Thread 57 beads onto yarn. With RS facing; join yarn with a slip st at upper edge of Flap (beginning chain), ready to work along side edge. Ch 1, work 33 bsc along side edge to point, work bsc at center point, work 33 bsc along remaining side to upper edge. Fasten off.

FINISHING

Using yarn needle, weave in all ends.

LINING

Using the Front as a pattern, cut 2 pieces of plastic canvas (Front and Back); cut a strip of plastic canvas the width and length of the Bottom and Side Gussets, piecing as necessary. Join the Back and Front plastic canvas pieces to the Bottom and Side Gussets piece, using an Overcast stitch. Set Lining aside.

ASSEMBLY

With wrong sides facing, pin Bottom and Side Gussets to Front, matching upper edges and easing to fit at lower corners. With RS facing, beginning at upper edge, join yarn with a slip st; working through both pieces, sc evenly down one side, across lower edge, and up opposite side to the upper edge. Fasten off. Repeat to join Bottom and Side Gussets to Back.

Place a marker at center of upper edge on Back; place a marker at center of straight edge of Flap (see Schematic). With RS facing, match center markers and pin Flap in place. Using smaller hook, join yarn at one edge of Flap and work a row slip st evenly across.

HANDLE CARRIERS
(MAKE 4; 2 EACH ON BACK AND FRONT)

Right-hand side: With RS facing, join yarn with a slip st, one st in from seam on upper edge.

Row 1: Ch 1, * sc in next 3 sts, turn—3 sc.

Continuing on these 3 sts, repeat Row 1 until piece measures 1 ¼"/3 cm from beginning. Fasten off, leaving a 12"/30.5 cm tail for sewing.

Thread carrier through opening at lower edge

of Purse handle; fold carrier to WS; using yarn needle threaded with tail, stitch end of carrier securely in place along upper edge of Purse.

Left-hand side: With RS facing, join yarn with a slip st, 4 sts in from left-hand seam on upper edge. Work as for right-hand side.

Insert Lining into Purse: whipstitch in place along upper edges of Back and Front.

EMBELLISHING

1. Cut a 12"/30.5 cm length of yarn and thread with 40 beads.

2. Tie end of yarn around Tassel neck, slide down the beads and wrap beaded yarn around neck of Tassel.

3. Secure yarn and thread through center of Tassel skirt. Fasten off.

4. Make Tassel loop: Cut a 1-yard/92 cm length of yarn and attach yarn to point of Flap; thread with 10 beads.

5. Work bc for 10 ch, thread chain through hanging cord of Tassel; join chain where it was attached. Weave in all ends.

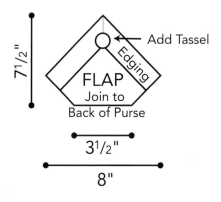

FLAP
Edging
Add Tassel
Join to
Back of Purse
7½"
3½"
8"

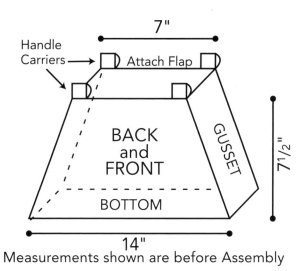

Handle Carriers
Attach Flap
7"
BACK and FRONT
GUSSET
BOTTOM
7½"
14"

Measurements shown are before Assembly

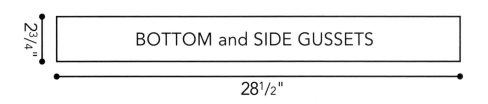

BOTTOM and SIDE GUSSETS
2¾"
28½"

Elegant Bolero Jacket

DESIGNED BY TREVA G. MCCAIN

EASY

This super-soft jacket is ideal for evening or day wear. The unique embellishing technique on this project creates a challenge for everyone to figure out how you added the beads and leaves them admiring the results.

SIZES

Small (Medium, Large)

FINISHED MEASUREMENTS

Chest 36 (38 ½, 40)"/91.5 (97.5, 101.5) cm

Length 20 ¾ (20 ¾, 22 ¼)"53 (53, 56.5) cm

YARN

Caron International's Simply Soft
(100% acrylic; 6 oz/170 g, 315 yds/288 m skein):

- #9703 Bone (MC), 2 (3, 3) skeins
- #9702 Off White (A), 1 skein

CROCHET HOOKS

One each size US I-9 (5.5 mm) and US J-10 (6 mm),
or size to obtain gauge

ADDITIONAL MATERIALS

Stitch markers

Yarn needle

Long-eye beading needle

100 Rectangle Mop Shell Component-Style Pure
Allure Beads (#370045)

Straight pins or small safety pins to use as markers

GAUGE

In Cluster-stitch pattern, 12 hdc clusters and 10 rows
= 4"/10 cm

CROCHET STITCHES USED

ch: chain

dc: double crochet

hdc: half double crochet

hdc3tog: half double crochet 3 together—[yarn over,
insert hook in st indicated and pull up a loop] twice,
yarn over and draw through 5 loops on hook.

sc: single crochet

sc2tog: single crochet 2 together—insert hook in next
st, yarn over and pull up a loop (2 loops on hook),
insert hook in next st, yarn over and pull up a loop,
yarn over and draw through all 3 loops on hook.

slip st: slip stitch

Cluster-stitch Pattern

- ROW 1: Inserting hook in third and fourth ch from
hook, hdc2tog (cluster made), * inserting hook in
same ch as last st, then in next ch, hdc2tog (cluster
made); repeat from * to end, turn.
- ROW 2: Ch 2, work cluster by inserting hook into
first and second cluster, * work cluster by inserting
hook in same place as last st, then in next cluster;
repeat from *, working last insertion in top of ch 2,
turn.
- Repeat Row 2 for Cluster-st.

NOTES

1. Cluster-st pattern looks the same on both sides,
therefore both Fronts are worked alike.

2. Bolero is meant to be worn open; there are no
buttons or closures.

BACK

Using smaller hook and MC, chain 56 (60, 62).

Row 1: Work Row 1 of Cluster-st—54, (58, 60) clusters.

Rows 2–30: Work even in Cluster-st, repeating Row 2.

SHAPE ARMHOLE

Row 1: Slip st in first 3 sts; ch 2, work cluster by inserting hook in same space as last slip st and in next st, continue in pattern across to last 3 sts, turn, leaving remaining sts unworked—48 (52, 54) clusters remain.

Row 2: Decrease Row—ch 2, hdc3tog over first 3 clusters, work in pattern across to last 3 st; hdc3tog over last 3 clusters, turn—46 (50, 52) clusters remain.

Rows 3 and 5: Work even in pattern (as Row 2 of Cluster-st.)

Row 4: Repeat Decrease Row—44 (48, 50) clusters remain.

Row 6: Repeat Decrease Row—42 (46, 48) clusters remain.

Rows 7–22 (22, 26): Work even in pattern. Fasten off.

FRONT (MAKE 2, BOTH ALIKE)

Using smaller hook and MC, chain 26 (28, 29).

Row 1: Work Row 1 of Cluster-st—24, (26, 27) clusters.

Rows 2–30: Work even in Cluster-st, repeating Row 2.

SHAPE ARMHOLE

Row 1: Continue in pattern across to last 3 sts, turn, leaving remaining sts unworked for underarm—21 (23, 24) clusters remain.

Row 2: Decrease Row—ch 2, hdc3tog over first 3 clusters, work in pattern to end—20 (22, 23) clusters remain.

Rows 3 and 5: Work even in pattern (as Row 2 of Cluster-st.)

Row 4: Repeat Decrease Row—19 (21, 22) clusters remain.

Row 6: Repeat Decrease Row—18 (20, 21) clusters remain.

Rows 7–11 (11, 15): Work even in pattern.

SHAPE NECK

Row 1: Work in pattern across to last 3 sts, turn, leaving remaining sts unworked for neck—15 (17, 18) clusters.

Row 2: Decrease Row—ch 2, hdc3tog over first 3 clusters, work in pattern to end, turn—14 (16, 17) clusters.

Rows 3, 5, and 7: Work even in pattern (as Row 2 of Cluster-st.)

Row 4: Repeat Decrease Row—13 (15, 16) clusters remain.

Row 6: Repeat Decrease Row—12 (14, 15) clusters remain.

Row 8: Repeat Decrease Row—11 (13, 14) clusters remain.

Rows 9–11: Work even in pattern. Fasten off.

SLEEVES (MAKE 2)

Using smaller hook and MC, chain 30 (30, 32).

Row 1: Work Row 1 of Cluster-st—28, (30, 30) clusters.

Rows 2 and 3: Work even in Cluster-st, repeating Row 2.

Row 4: Increase Row—ch 2, work cluster by inserting hook in ch-2 space and first cluster; continue in pattern across to last st, work 2 clusters in last st—30 (30, 32) clusters.

Rows 5–7, 9–11 and 13–15: Work even in pattern.

Row 8: Repeat Increase Row—32 (32, 34) clusters.

Row 12: Repeat Increase Row—34, (34, 36) clusters.

Row 16: Repeat Increase Row—36 (36, 38) clusters.

Rows 17–32: Work even in pattern.

SHAPE CAP

Row 1: Slip st in first 4 sts; ch 2, work cluster by inserting hook in same space as last slip st and in next st, work in pattern across to last 3 clusters, turn, leaving remaining sts unworked—30 (30, 32) clusters remain.

Row 2: Decrease Row—ch 2, hdc3tog over first 3 clusters, work in pattern across to last 3 st; hdc3tog over last 3 clusters, turn—28 (28, 30) clusters remain.

Row 3: Work even in pattern (as Row 2 of Cluster-st.)

Rows 4–18: Repeat Decrease Row every other row eight times more, ending with a Decrease Row—12 (12, 14) clusters remain. Fasten off.

FINISHING

Using yarn needle and MC, sew shoulder seams, set in Sleeves, sew side and underarm seams.

BOLERO EDGING

Round 1: With RS facing, using larger hook and MC, join yarn with a slip st at right Front side seam; ch 1, working in remaining loops of beginning ch, sc in same space, sc evenly across to lower right Front corner; work 3 sc in next st (corner), place a marker in the center of these 3 sc; [work 2 sc in each row-rnd] to neck edge; work corner, pm; sc in each of next 2 sc; repeat from [to] to right shoulder seam; sc in each st across to left shoulder seam; repeat from [to] to beginning of neck shaping; sc in each of next 2 sc; work corner, pm; repeat from [to] to lower left Front corner; work corner, pm; working in remaining loops of beginning ch, work across to right Front seam, join with a slip st to beginning sc, changing to CC in last st before joining.

SHAPE NECK EDGING

Rounds 2 and 3: Using CC, ch 1, sc in same space and in each st across to marked corner st, work 3 sc in marked st, moving marker to the center of these 3 sc (corner); sc in each st to next marker; work corner; sc in each of the next 2 sts, sc2tog over next 2 st (decrease), sc in each st across to 4 sts before next marker; sc2tog over next 2 st, sc in each of the next 2 sts; work corner; sc in each st to next marked st, work corner; sc in each st around to beginning, join with a slip st to beginning sc, changing to MC in last st of Round 3 before joining.

Rounds 4 and 5: Using MC, ch 1, sc in same space and in each st around, working 3 sc in each marked corner st.

Round 6: Using MC, ch 1, sc in same space, ch 1, * sc in next sc, ch 1; repeat from * around; join with a slip st to beginning sc.

SLEEVE EDGING

Round 1: With RS facing, using larger hook and MC, join yarn with a slip st at sleeve seam; ch 1, working in the remaining loops of beginning ch, sc in same space and in each ch around; join with a slip st to beginning sc.

Round 2: Ch 1, sc in same space and in each sc around, join with a slip st to beginning sc, changing to A in last st before joining.

Rounds 3 and 4: Using A, work even in sc (as for Round 2), changing to MC in last st of Round 4.

Rounds 5 and 6: Using MC, work even in sc.

Round 7: Using MC, ch 1, sc in same space, ch 1, * sc in next sc, ch 1; repeat from * around, join with a slip st to beginning sc. Weave in all ends.

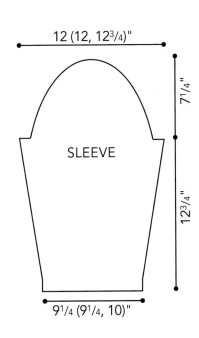

EMBELLISHING

BEADING

1. Separate 4-ply yarn into 2-ply strand (See page 15).

2. Place pins as markers approx 1"/2.5 cm apart for bead placement.

3. Attach yarn on WS of jacket where first bead is to be attached.

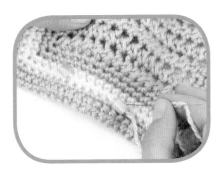

4. Bring yarn through to RS, draw yarn through bead, sliding bead down to jacket.

5. Leaving enough space for the bead to lie flat, insert needle through jacket border to WS as shown in photo above.

6. On the WS, slide the needle through the inside of the stitches of the jacket border up to where the next bead should be placed.

7. Repeat Steps 5 and 6 until all beads have been attached.

3³/₄ (4¹/₄, 4³/₄)"

6¹/₂"

4¹/₄"

8³/₄ (8³/₄, 10¹/₄)"

20³/₄ (20³/₄, 22¹/₄)"

BACK AND LEFT FRONT

12"

8 (8¹/₂, 9)"

18 (19¹/₄, 20)"

12 (12, 12³/₄)"

7¹/₄"

SLEEVE

12³/₄"

9¹/₄ (9¹/₄, 10)"

resources

Caron International

PO Box 222
Washington, NC 27889
800 868 9194

www.caron.com
www.shopcaron.com

Bead Crazy (for Myuki beads in Cropped Vest)

21 Taft Corners Shopping Center
Williston, VT 05495
802 228 9666

www.beadcrazyvt.com

The Beadery (for African-motif beads used in
Sahara Shawl, pony beads used in Flower Wrap,
and others)

PO Box 178
Hope Valley, RI 02832
401 539 2432

www.thebeadery.com

Cousin Corp (for miracle beads used in
Beaded Ruffled Shrug and others)

PO Box 2939
Largo, FL 22779
727 536 3568

www.cousin.com

Darice, Inc (for rocaille and seed beads used
in Boho Bangles and others)

13000 Darice Parkway, Park 82
Strongsville, OH 44149
866 432 7423

www.darice.com

Fire Mountain Gems (for beads used in
Midnight Duster, Evening Capelet, and others)

One Fire Mountain Way
Grants Pass, OR 97526-2373
800 355 2137

www.firemountaingems.com

Pure Allure (for shell and crystal beads used
in Elegant Bolero Jacket and others)

4005 Avenida De La Plata
Oceanside, CA 92056
800 536 6312

www.pureallure.com

glossary

CROCHET STITCHES

Chain (ch): Begin by making a slip knot on your hook. * Wrap the yarn around the hook (yarn over) and pull up a loop [draw the yarn through the loop on the hook to form the first chain]. Repeat from * for number of chains required. Note: The loop on the hook is not included when counting the number of chains.

Cluster: A group of stitches worked together for decorative purposes, instead of to decrease; work as instructions indicate.

Double Crochet (dc): Yarn over hook, insert hook into stitch indicated, yarn over and pull up a loop, [yarn over and draw through two loops on hook] twice.

Double Treble Crochet (dtr): Yarn over hook three times, insert hook into stitch indicated, yarn over and pull up a loop, [yarn over and draw through two loops] four times.

Half Double Crochet (hdc): Yarn over hook, insert hook into stitch indicated, yarn over and pull up a loop, yarn over and draw through all three loops on hook.

Picot: A decorative edge pattern stitch used for edgings; work as instructions indicate.

Shell: A number of stitches worked into one stitch for decorative purposes instead of to increase; work as instructions indicate.

Single Crochet (sc): Insert hook in stitch indicated, yarn over and pull up a loop, yarn over and draw through both loops on hook.

Slip Stitch (slip st): Insert hook in the stitch indicated, yarn over and draw through both the stitch and the loop on the hook.

Treble Crochet (tr): Yarn over hook two times, insert hook in stitch indicated, yarn over and pull up a loop, [yarn over and draw through two loops] three times.

SPECIAL TERMS AND ABBREVIATIONS

dc2tog (single decrease): Double crochet 2 together—[Yarn over, insert hook in next stitch, yarn over and pull up a loop, yarn over and draw through 2 loops on hook] twice, yarn over and draw through all 3 loops on hook.

dc3tog (double decrease): Double crochet 3 together—[Yarn over, insert hook in next stitch, yarn over and pull up a loop, yarn over and draw through 2 loops on hook] 3 times, yarn over and draw through all 4 loops on hook.

dec: Decrease—work 2 (or the number indicated in the instructions) stitches together *in pattern* unless instructed otherwise.

FPdc: Front-post double crochet: (RS) Yarn over, insert hook from right-hand side of stitch to WS of piece, return to RS at left-hand side of stitch indicated, yarn over and pull up loop, returning to starting point, complete as dc.

hdc2tog (single decrease): Half double crochet 2 together—[Yarn over, insert hook in next st and pull up a loop] twice, yarn over and draw through 5 loops on hook.

inc: Increase—work 2 (or the number indicated in the instructions) stitches into the next stitch.

sc2tog (single decrease): Single crochet 2 together—[Insert hook in next stitch, yarn over and pull up a loop] twice, yarn over and draw through all 3 loops on hook.

sc3tog (double decrease): Single crochet 3 together—[Insert hook in next stitch, yarn over and pull up a loop] 3 times, yarn over and draw through all 4 loops on hook.

slip st 2tog (single decrease): Slip stitch 2 together—Insert hook in next st, yarn over and pull up a loop, insert hook in next st, yarn over and draw through st and loops on hook.

SPECIAL TECHNIQUES

Base Chain/Single Crochet (Base ch/sc) **NOTE: This technique creates a foundation chain and a row of sc at the same time.**

- **FIRST STITCH**
  Begin with a slip knot; ch 2, insert hook into second ch from hook, * yarn over and pull up a loop, yo and draw through one loop (this is the chain), yo and draw through 2 loops (this is the sc).

- **NEXT STITCH:**
  NOTE: The next st is worked under the forward 2 loops of the stem of the previous st (the chain) made when working the st. Insert hook into the bottom of the previous st, under 2 loops, repeat from * of first st. Repeat this step for number of sts indicated in instructions.

Bead Crochet: **See Basic Techniques (page 12).**

Tunisian Crochet/Afghan Stitch (any number of stitches) **NOTE: Each row of Tunisian Crochet is worked in two steps.**

- **FOUNDATION ROW (counts as Step 1 for first Row only)**
  Chain the number of sts indicated in the instructions.
  Skip the first chain, * insert hook in second chain from hook, yarn over and pull up a loop (2 loops on hook); repeat from * across, pulling up a loop in each chain. Complete Foundation Row by working Step 2 (below).

- **STEP 1:** With RS facing, working from right to left, pick up the stitches:
  Beginning in the second vertical bar of the previous row, * insert hook into the vertical bar, yarn over and draw a loop through the vertical bar (2 loops on hook); repeat from * across, drawing up a loop in each vertical bar.

- **STEP 2:** With RS facing, working from left to right, work off the stitches:
  Yarn over and draw through first loop on hook, * yarn over and draw through 2 loops on hook; repeat from * across.

- Repeat Steps 1 and 2 for Tunisian Crochet.

metric conversion

Inches to cm = 2.54

Yards to Meters = .92

Meters to Yards = 1.08

Oz to Grams = 28.6

40g = 1.4 oz   25g = .88 oz

BUST		LENGTH	
INS	CM	INS	CM
½" add 1 — ¾" add 2			
30	76	10	25
31	78.5	11	28
32	81	12	30.5
33	84	13	33
34	86.5	14	35.5
35	89	15	38
36	91.5	16	40.5
37	94	17	43
38	96.5	18	45.5
39	99	19	48
40	101.5	20	51
41	104	21	53.5
42	106.5	22	56
43	109	23	58.5
44	112	24	61
45	114	25	63.5
46	117	26	66
47	119	27	68.5
48	122	28	71
49	124.5	29	73.5
50	127		
51	129.5		
52	132		
53	134.5		
54	137		
55	139.5		
56	142		
57	145		
58	147.5		
59	150		
60	152		
61	155		
62	157.5		
63	160		
64	162.5		
65	165		

index